WHAT THE RELIGIOUS REVOLUTIONARIES ARE SAYING

ELWYN A. SMITH

Editor

FORTRESS PRESS

Philadelphia

Library of Congress Catalog Card Number 72–155949

ISBN 0–8006–0133–5

1592H71   Printed in U.S.A.   1–133

TABLE OF CONTENTS

2.79

Baker & Taylor

23 April 73

47474

FOREWORD

The sight of a man in a clerical collar standing in the front line of a demonstration is deeply puzzling to many Americans. What are these ministers, priests, and rabbis thinking about? How can they mix their spiritual calling with social agitation?

This short book gives the "religious revolutionaries," as we have termed them, an opportunity to explain their views on the drug culture, abortion, "black theology"—on about a dozen key issues. Not all the questions that intrigue you are debated here, but by reading these discussions you may be able to discern the general trend of their thoughts, for the religious revolutionaries do share an approach to faith and social responsibility. That is why there are two articles in this book about "doing theology." All these writers are and want to be theological; they are aware of their historical roots in religion. But to them, theology is not speculation or theory, but something they *do.* In this book you will see them at work and perhaps begin to grasp their approach to the great question of what believers ought to do about their faith. What is genuinely revolutionary about them is the way they connect belief with action; to understand that is to understand the religious revolution.

E. A. S.

Philadelphia, Pennsylvania
January 1971

HOLY ORDERS
AND UNHOLY DISORDERS

JOSEPH C. WILLIAMSON

The subject of this essay is focused on by an assignment I faced in the spring of 1970. I had accepted the invitation of a theological student and friend to preach at his service of ordination. My intention was to use the theme of "holy orders" to show that God's ordering of nature and history had been disrupted by the unholy disordering of man, a disordering which was camouflaged beneath a presidential call for "law and order."

During the week before I was to preach, there occurred first the invasion into Cambodia and then the invasion into Kent State and Jacksonville State by the United States military. The camouflage was shredded, the realities exposed. The agents of "law and order" were in fact the perpetrators of lawlessness and disorder. In the chaos of that disorder it was my responsibility as a theologian to articulate what "holy orders" ought to mean both for the nation and for those who claim to be the church of Jesus Christ. That is a presumptuous task, but it is the risk theologians must take. In other words, to do theology is to seek to discern and articulate those normative patterns of order which both judge the disordered lives and institutions of mankind and at the same time point us toward the realization of a new and holy order where justice, peace, and

1

freedom are established. Among the plethora of academic "sciences," theology is the one discipline which *necessarily* is required to take this risk. Other disciplines may do this. John Seeley, for instance, has argued such a case for sociology. But theology has no option. It must do this if it is to remain theology. That is also why theology ought particularly in an abnormative and disordered world to be a revolutionary enterprise.

Now, the obvious fact is that those who claim to be theologians rarely do their work in a revolutionary way. We prefer the accumulation of footnotes and the citation of Latin phrases. We are fascinated with ideas but we are generally unwilling to test those ideas in the streets of the suburbs or the ghetto. We engage in debates, like the one at the 1969 meeting of the American Academy of Religion, on the relationship between philosophy and theology, which could have taken place in the thirteenth century for all the apparent lack of interest in accounting for changes in historical climate or social soil. Those discussions may be interesting, but when they are abstracted from the material realities of the world in which we live they are diversionary rather than revolutionary.

At one stage in my own religious movement I thought that theology was in trouble because it was required to speak of God. Since so-called modern man cannot accept the premise of a transcendent reality, I became increasingly diffident in my vocational role. Harvey Cox called for a moratorium on God-talk as one way out of our dilemma. William Hamilton, spokesman for the "radicals," proclaimed the "death of God." That phase I now see as an incorrect solution to a mis-identified problem. Theology failed, not because it spoke of God, but because the God of whom it spoke was unrelated to the world in which men and women lived. In other words, the crucial question for us is not posed by Freud. It is not the problem of "the future of an illusion" with which we ought to be concerned.

Rather, the question which demands hearing and answering is set by Marx. Theology has become suspect for largely the same reasons that the philosophical idealism of Hegel became suspect. The ideal is separated from the real. God is separated from the world. The basic problem is the abstraction of the theological "mind" from the theological "body," which is to say, the material realities of human existence. Because of this abstraction the integrity of the whole enterprise is questioned. We must find a way to pursue the theological task in which the normative symbols of the discipline are necessarily related to the abnormative state of affairs in which our society exists. Only if this relationship can be sustained is it possible to speak of a theology which is informed by and serviceable to those who regard themselves as religious revolutionaries.

I wish now to set out five criteria for doing this kind of theology. They are not put forth with any particular kind of logic. As a matter of fact, they are so interrelated, so mixed-up with each other, that it is not possible to ascribe priority to any one. Nor can I offer a finally persuasive defense for choosing these five characteristics. They emerge out of the matrix of biblical materials, historical consciousness, and personal experience which has informed my own theological development. In that sense they do represent my confession of faith. But that faith is not merely mine. It is shaped to a large extent in the context of that community of persons who share this way of seeing and living. No theologian can go about his task on his own. His work is necessarily done in and for the fellowship of those who both catch his vision and are willing to challenge it. At best, my responsibility is to serve as a catalytic agent within the mixtures of solutions and dissolutions where I work. Sometimes the catalysis is helpful, sometimes not. Judgment about that must be kept open.

The first mark of a revolutionary theology is that it must draw its vitality from the taproot of religion. Any form of intellectual activity tends to isolate itself from the raw materials of human experience. Theology is not immune from such a tendency. The university has been criticized recently by Theodore Roszak for perpetuating what he terms "technical rationality," that form of intellectual activity which splits off reason from life. Roszak maintains that the primary question we must face is not the question "How do we know?" but the question "How do we live?" In the context of this discussion, that way of putting the prior question indicates that the theological or intellectual formulation must always be dependent upon the religious realities which invigorate and impel us. Of course, religion is a multiform phenomenon. Dietrich Bonhoeffer proposed in his *Letters and Papers from Prison* what he called "religionless Christianity." I am (in what appears to be a contradiction) in sympathy with much of what Bonhoeffer says. But that sympathy is possible only because of the peculiar definition of *religion* which he employs. By *religion* I do not mean the sacralization of the universe, nor do I mean the appeal to God as the cosmic solver of the human predicament. Rather, by the religious dimensions of life I intend to indicate two fundamental realities: first, the religious is expressed in those emotions or passions or affections which haunt, threaten, enliven, and motivate us; second, the religious is also represented in the organization of those emotions into collective patterns, symbols, and rituals which affirm a coherent meaning and purpose for life. I shall elaborate the substance of these two dimensions.

It is almost a cliché to observe that the Western intellectual tradition has developed in such a way as to force the separation of the intellect or "mind" from the passions or "heart." There are exceptions within that tradition. Jonathan Edwards in colonial America and Søren Kierkegaard in nineteenth-century Europe were two theologians who notably resisted such a separation. But it is precisely the fact that they were so exceptional which distinguishes them. What theology needs if it is to be revolutionary is to get in touch again with those fundamental emotions which are surging among us. Take, for instance, the passion of outrage. The liberal critics who oppose the unrespectable tactics of ghetto rebellions or the burning of the Bank of America decry such activity as being an "irrational" demand for social change. What they fail to perceive is that the outrage expressed in such activity has a quality of human passion about it that expresses authentic religious realities. In the face of the sterile and demeaning rationalities set by the established orders of American society, such outrage may indeed assume an "irrational" form. But that madness is also a sign of life.

Or, take the passion of ecstasy. The religion of the American churches is counterecstatic. Has anyone ever become excited singing the Gloria Patri? Has anyone ever danced to the doxology? Religion without ecstasy is predictably formal and ordered. That may keep some people in their place, but that place is a miserable state of affairs. Recently in New York City a prominent rock group was told by the authorities policing their outdoor concert that the time for closing had passed. The group insisted on playing again. The electricity was cut off. Then, without amplification, the group began to play "Amazing Grace," and the audience rose to their feet and began to sing until the volume of unison voices resounded higher than even the electrified sound. Imagine that message for the people of New York:

> I once was lost, but now I'm found,
> Was blind, but now I see.

The vitality of religious ecstasy has passed out of the Cathedral of Saint John the Divine, but it is still alive in the sheepmeadow of Central Park. That vitality must inform the theology of authentic religion.

It is true, of course, that raw emotions can disintegrate into destructive chaos. That disintegration must be resisted by the organization of the passions into patterns of meaning which express a transcending purpose of life. The cry for relevance in religion is partly a cry for immediacy, but it is also an expression of deep longing for the affirmation that the center does after all hold. It is not necessary to detail at length the evacuation of power from the traditional symbols of Christianity. It is not necessary to rehearse here the way in which those symbols have been co-opted under the aegis of American civil religion. What is important is the emerging realization among those who regard themselves as religious revolutionaries that dramatic signs, both old and new, are serving as sources of identity and pride for their particular community of faith.

In Boston on The Day After, following the verdicts given to the men charged with "conspiracy" to incite to riot at the 1968 Democratic convention, the old symbol of the cross was carried down Tremont Street by a group whose discipleship of Jesus of Nazareth required them to express their commitment to the forces of life against the principalities and powers of repression and death in that way. It was not incongruous but appropriate that the litany they chanted as they marched was "Off the pig." The convergence of the old and the new on that particular march did reinvigorate both the demonstrators and the symbolic burden they carried on their backs. No theology which is not bound up with these kinds of religious manifestations will be adequate for our movement through the social turmoil of our lives.

The second mark of a revolutionary theology is that it must be integrally related to the material realities of human existence. I have already indicated my conviction that the charge of "irrelevance" becomes appropriate to theology whenever that relationship is not sustained. It is illegitimate, for example, to speak of "spiritual" emancipation from the bondage of sin without speaking at the same time of "material" emancipation from the demonic political and economic forces which enslave the oppressed peoples of the world. Keeping the spiritual and the material realities together is what the exodus of Israel from Egypt was about. That is also what the Freedom Movement of black people in America is about. To put this challenge aphoristically, we must set about doing for theology what Marx did for Hegel; that is, we must flesh out the vocabulary of faith with what is actually happening in our lives. To those who are familiar with the substance of Christianity such a mandate should come as no surprise. It is the necessary implication of the confession that God is to be known not at the end of a philosophical argument but in the particular life of a particular man known as Jesus of Nazareth, and in the community of those who follow him. Incarnation means making the Word flesh and blood. The "Word" is not an idea abstracted from life. That "Word" can be heard and responded to only insofar as it is a fully human word which is articulated in the context of a fully human world.

Most of the time, however, we do not take this mandate seriously. The world of the classroom and the world of God become isolated from the world of economic exploitation and the world where genocide is carried out against the red and black and yellow peoples. Piety divorced from politics becomes another occasion for mystification, for doublethink and double-talk. Robert Bly sets the truth for us in one of his poems when he claims "the two worlds are both in this world." The two worlds are not collapsed into one-dimensionality. Transcendence is not forfeited. But the two worlds must be present at the same time in the one world where people struggle for their lives and where they face the daily threat of suffering and death. Fortunately a few theological voices have been raised to make this clear. This is what the American black man James Cone does in *Black Theology and Black Power*. This is what the Brazilian Protestant Rubem Alves contends for in *A Theology for Human Hope*. Even more significant, this is the kind of theology which Bobby Seale expresses in his narration of the development of the Black Panther party. "Faith," he says, "is not a mythical bullshit thing. Faith is where you directly relate yourself to reality."[1] Faith and theological reflection upon that faith must each relate themselves to the reality of the world. That much is incontrovertible.

Given the two preceding assumptions, the third mark of a theological effort which claims to be revolutionary in intention is that it proceeds by an act of negation or judgment upon the present worldly state of affairs. The first word to be spoken in the dialectic of redemption is always an indictment. One thing which characterizes both theology and revolution is that they necessarily reject the definition of what is declared as normative according to the established criteria of the status quo. For Americans this means that neither the success-oriented values of our culture nor the exploitative social system which sustains the realization of those values can be tolerated. Both must be drastically transformed, and that transformation cannot proceed according to the gratuitous favors dispensed by those who control the mechanisms of this society. This claim runs counter to the whole socialization process by which our lives have been conditioned. We have been taught to deny our revolutionary heritage. Teachers in certain public schools have been instructed to refer to the "War for Independence" rather than to the "Revolutionary War." The intention is clear: Keep the children under wraps by cheating on the truth. But all the last-ditch efforts at control are beginning to disintegrate. The message of *Catch 22* is catching on. The society is not normal but abnormal. Sanity is attained not by adjustment but by rebellion. The vocabulary of those who seek autonomy and individuality is stocked with negatives. They cry a resounding "No."

That cry always comes as a shock to those against whom it is spoken. But religious folk should not be so surprised. The prophetic lineage by which we trace our own identities maintains that tearing down must always come before the building up. Crucifixion is the precondition for resurrection. Death to the old is required if there is to be life to the new. One of the most important saints in the hagiography of the emerging church is Father Daniel Berrigan. He was, to use Paul Cowan's phrase, a "fugitive from injustice," living underground, wanted by the F.B.I. to serve his three-and-a-half year sentence for napalming the selective service files at Catonsville, Maryland. Recently Father Berrigan has been saying that "resistance," or negation, must not be taken as a temporary strategy for opposing a particular governmental policy such as the American war in Southeast Asia. Rather, resistance must become for us a total way of life. War is not a "mistake" in the otherwise successful history of the nation. Instead, that war is the full revelation of what the true nature of American imperialism actually is. It is the whole range of oppression and exploitation by this country which must be resisted.

This brings us to the fourth mark of that theology which may be of service to those of us who regard ourselves as religious revolutionaries. To negate the negative is at the same time to affirm the possibility of that new reality which lies beyond us. Negation is not nihilism. Negation of war is the affirmation of peace. Negation of repression is the affirmation of freedom. The second word to be spoken in the dialectic of redemption is the word of affirmation and of promise. It is the word which pushes us from the immobility of history's "dead center" where we find ourselves toward the horizons of a future where hope becomes a possibility again. It is still true that "without a vision the people perish." With that vision, that expectation, that lure, the people live. And where is the vision to be found? Is it in the cynicism of those Americans who fight in Vietnam? Or is it in the tenacious struggle of those Asian peoples who refuse to cease in their resistance to a war machine that has defoliated an area of land now larger than the state of Massachusetts?

This expectation of a new and open future, this promise of the resurrection which defies the sealed tombs created by our national brutality, is informed by the radically eschatological character of biblical faith. Recently, Jürgen Moltmann and others have affirmed that this is the distinctive element which sets the Judeo-Christian tradition apart from all the other ways of seeing life. For me, the realization of this quality came not while reading Schweitzer's famous thesis but in the act of seeing Passolini's film, *The Gospel According to Saint Matthew*. There, without interpolation, without piety, the biblical text broke through its numb familiarity and came alive. Jesus of Nazareth was no sedentary Christ. He was on the move into that future of the reign of God. For us to catch that sense of movement our imaginations must be freed from all pragmatic and restricting conventionalities. Why *not* eroticize the full range of human experience so that all the senses throb? Why *not* liquidate all the bank accounts and properties of churches so that the poor might have the money Rockefeller gave to "God"? Dream those kinds of dreams and see those kinds of visions and let the promises be fulfilled.

The fifth and final mark for doing theology this way is that it must be worked out within the context of the community which shares this faith. I have already indicated my convictions concerning this. Of course, that community which is now taking shape cannot be defined by the existing ecclesiastical institutions. The religious vitalities which we cherish move outside those structures. Things are happening to bring us together in new and different ways. We are finding the power of a shared vocabulary. If "all power is given to the people," then the meek shall inherit the earth. We are learning the importance of nurturing one another. Support and tenderness are being given. We are taking seriously the need for discipline, not just perpetuating the Protestant heresy of "doing our own thing." When theology is done in corporate ways then it cannot be an esoteric trick bag of intellectual riddles. It will be of help only as that new community becomes a stay against the chaos of the world, a place where brothers and sisters laugh and cry together, a base for movement into all the struggles that we face.

I began by saying that to be a theologian means to articulate the normative patterns of life for the people of God in an abnormative world. That means making certain claims about the substance of righteousness and truth. I understand the folly of such claims. But I also understand the folly of the present hour, an hour which is almost up. It is past time for us to "seize the time."

NOTES

1. *Seize the Time* (New York: Random House, 1970), p. 104.

AMERICAN POWER AND
THE POWERLESS NATIONS

RICHARD SHAULL

It does not require a prophet to predict that the main problem the United States will confront in its international relations during the remaining decades of this century will not be that of getting along with the powerful countries of the world but rather that of working out a new relationship with the powerless nations of Asia, Africa, and Latin America.

We have already discovered that some sort of *modus vivendi* with Russia is possible; before too long, we may begin to work one out with China. But no such encouraging prospects are in store for us in relation to the peoples of the Third World. These peoples, like the blacks and other minority groups in our own society, are discovering that they are victimized and powerless. For centuries a basically colonial structure has deprived them of a significant role in international affairs, has imposed on them economic, political, and social structures which are alien to their own culture and history, and has taken economic advantage of them while they have remained poor. It is this situation as a whole which their new consciousness finds intolerable. We, the United States of America, appear as the main bulwark of the status quo.

Not everyone, of course, in the nations of the Third

World, is aware of all this or reacts in this way. But the new nationalism is already a powerful force, and it is likely to become much more widespread and to increase in intensity in the years ahead. Moreover, the nationalist demand is being expressed in terms which are loud and clear: freedom to develop their own institutions and structures and to go their own way; the opportunity to be masters of their own economic destiny and to use their resources for their own benefit; and some significant participation in decisions on the international plane about war and peace, economic order, and trade, which inevitably affect them.

To take these demands seriously would require radical changes in our present policy, changes which, it is assumed, would threaten our security, diminish our power, and lower our standard of living. For us to accept them seems completely out of the question. Thus the power of our system is used to preserve the main lines of the present relationship, even though (as is the case with the war in Indochina) it means the expenditure of vast amounts of money, the radical altering of our national priorities, massive destruction of life and property, and the alienation of the most sensitive and concerned of a new generation.

The one significant political group which attempts to offer an alternative wants us to get out of Vietnam, cut back our military involvements elsewhere, increase economic aid and technical assistance to the poor nations, etc. But by and large it hopes to improve the situation *without fundamentally altering the structures of our relationship to the nations of the Third World,* an alteration which the new nationalists in these countries consider essential in order to move beyond the present impasse. The limited number of individuals and groups who advocate and are working for a more radical shift have no real political power and little hope of getting it.

What the Religious Revolutionaries Are Saying

What then lies ahead for us? It may well be that our nation will fail to respond to this challenge, become more and more threatened by the mounting pressures for change, and attempt to maintain its position by military means as well as by more subtle forms of domination. Such a Pax Americana could continue for a long time. But the price we and the world will have to pay for it will be terrifying: the intensification of bitterness and hatred on the part of the dispossessed; the indefinite postponement of efforts to find creative solutions to urgent economic, social, and political problems in the developing nations; and the proliferation of attempts at revolt and revolution on the part of those who are desperate, with all the bloodshed this would involve.

For those of us who cannot sit idly by and await the advent of such an apocalypse, there is, I believe, another possibility open. It is that of a *long-term effort which aims at the transformation of consciousness and builds, on that foundation, new forms of political pressure and action in relation to our foreign policy*. To take on this overwhelming task we need not be convinced that we are going to succeed. But we do need to wager that people can face new realities in their world, call into question their present attitudes and perspectives, move to a new understanding, and discover resources for new types of action. And we will be forced to explore ways by which this can happen and to do so in association with others who are committed to a similar task.

In recommending this, we are not inventing a utopian scheme but rather speaking of something that has begun to happen spontaneously, even though on a very small scale in various parts of the country. Groups of young people, many of them returned volunteers (from the Peace Corps or mission organizations), have come together to work at specific tasks. Some are engaging in research on how American power operates in Latin America, Africa, or Asia, making the results of their investigations available to a variety of movements and organizations. Others are developing projects which combine study and action, and are seeking for ways to involve others in them. Still others are exploring ways by which Americans who have traveled to Asia, Africa, or Latin America begin to work out the implications of their recent discoveries, arrive at new levels of understanding, and find new possibilities of action.

As these young people go about this work and pay the price it demands they draw their resources for the struggle from many different places. I happen to focus my attention, in these efforts, on the Christian faith because it has been one of the major sources for my perspective on life and the world and has provided me with the possibilities I have found for living a process of transformation or communicating it to others. In spite of what I see in the church, I discover that I am part of a historical community of faith that has come to the surface at rare and unexpected moments in the past. When this community has appeared, it has given expression, in thought and action, to an unusual approach to life and the world. It has affirmed that life reaches its greatest fulfillment not when we hold on to the old order and its logic, but when we break with it and risk creating the new; that life is open to a qualitatively new future and that we can expect to be surprised by new possibilities; that by participating in a constant ongoing process of transformation we can reverse the natural tendency toward sclerosis, decay, and death, and move toward an expanding life of increased meaning and fulfillment. What has been even more surprising, at rare moments, is the fact that such communities have discovered that this can happen not only in their personal existence but also within the structures of the world. When institutions, movements, and nations are free to give up old structures that have lost their capacity to provide meaningful human relationships, abandon old perspectives which no longer deal adequately with new realities, and risk new responses to new challenges, they open the way to new forms of social stability and greater possibilities of justice. In fact, by such creative action, they make a new future possible not only for the dispossessed and powerless but often also for those who have most profited from the old order and thus appeared to have most to lose by its collapse.

In the past, this experience has been described and interpreted by a particular set of theological terms: the sovereignty of God and his action in history; the initiation of a new order in the world through the resurrection of Christ and the eschatological expectation of its fulfillment; the apocalyptic understanding of God's judgment on the world as the occasion for the inbreaking of a new order, etc. For most people outside the church and even for many within, this language is no longer the bearer of a new social vision or of power for transformation. But I happen to believe in this perspective on reality and the experience of life which it describes and want to see that operative in people's lives today; I am, moreover, confident, in spite of all the evidence to the contrary, that there are quite a few people in the church or on the margin of it who are willing to risk putting such a way of life to the test. I would wager that, if and when they do so, they will also be surprised to discover resources for it in the experience of the historical community out of which they have come.

My concern, therefore, for the future of our relations as a nation to the Third World leads me to concentrate on searching out and helping to create such communities of transformation. Other people, in the church, will choose other approaches, and I hope they will be successful. But I have lost all faith in the power of moral exhortation from the pulpits or in church pronouncements to the world. As a result of long experience with various ecclesiastical organizations and in the ecumenical movement, I expect very little to come from efforts to educate and mobilize the church constituency for action in this sphere; and I think that the time is long since past when the church, as an institution in American society, can hope to play a significant role in shaping our foreign policy in the direction of radical change. But I am interested in doing all I can to encourage small groups of men and women, concerned about our relation to the Third World, to get together in order to question their present attitudes toward what is happening in the world, explore alternative approaches, and make use of all means at their disposal to create a new base for political action.

To the extent that such communities emerge, Christian faith will help to create a small ferment in our society which may be of significance in the years ahead. In this way, it would be able to provide models for the process of transformation of consciousness and for new forms of political action; it could also introduce into society a constant critical approach to the present order of relations and the assumptions behind them. It might even provide some new clues for understanding the task of our nation at the end of the colonial era and suggest concrete proposals for working out that new relationship. Within this framework, those of us who are working at the theological task will not spend our time formulating Christian principles or "middle axioms" for international affairs, nor will we be tempted to become amateur political scientists or radical politicians. But we may discover that our theological resources make it possible for us to be constantly raising critical questions and suggesting new directions, both to those engaged in more theoretical work and to the new political activities. I would here like to suggest briefly some possibilities which I see in relation to several central issues we now face in our confrontation with the Third World.

(1) People in the new nations have come to a fresh awareness of the particularity and richness of their own cultural heritage and situation and are convinced that they can be authentically themselves only as they develop institutions and structures that take their own culture seriously. Thus far we have seen this desire as a threat to us and have often tried to thwart its realization. Why should we not rather recognize in it an unusual opportunity not only for the development of those countries but also for ourselves? The vitality of our own institutions has been due, in large part, to our insistence that we had to do precisely the same thing in response to our situation and hopes, rather than import obsolete structures from Europe. And our willingness to permit and encourage the same process in other parts of the world, at a new juncture in history, would open the way to a new future not only for those nations but perhaps for us as well.

To encourage and profit from this would indeed require quite a transformation of consciousness on our part. It would mean that we would have to take a long and critical look at the many manifestations of our cultural imperialism. We would recognize the absurdity of sending experts in education to Brazil to reform their educational system at a time when our own educational institutions are in crisis and when the results of new pedagogical experiments in Brazil are providing new insights and possibilities for many in Europe and America. It would mean that we recognize the futility of imposing our economic, political, and social systems on countries where conditions are very different from ours and whose background does not lead them in the same direction. When our "democratic" institutions are exported to South Vietnam, for example, they undergo radical transformation and produce something quite different from what we expect. Further, it would mean that we would have to overcome, once and for all, the *paternalism* which is so evident in our relationships to the Third World. We have now reached, perhaps for the first time in human history, a position in which rich and poor, strong and weak, those of different races, cultures, and nations, can and must relate to each other on the basis of equality. To recognize that fact, and develop patterns of relationship consistent with it, might lead to new forms of mutuality in the midst of wide differences which would not only bring promise for international peace and stability, but stimulate us all to seek new and better options for a society open to the future.

(2) In the economic sphere, the change demanded of us in face of the new realities is perhaps greater than anywhere else. The people of Asia, Africa, and Latin America want economic development to occur as rapidly as possible. We assume that the way to achieve it is by the adoption of the system we have developed in the past hundred years and by close association with the dynamics of our expanding economy as it reaches abroad. The people of the Third World do not agree. They are convinced that this option has failed them at two points which are most important for them. First, they naturally assume that their country should choose its own economic goals and decide how to achieve them; that as far as possible it should be master of its own economic household. But what they see happening is the opposite of this. To the extent that they develop in the direction of corporate capitalism, they are caught by

19

a structure of development which makes it increasingly impossible for them to achieve the goals they have set; they find, further, that the greater their development, the more dependent their country becomes on the United States as it is integrated into our economic sphere of influence. Secondly, since in their countries a small minority have great wealth and a high percentage live in extreme poverty, they are committed to a type of economic development which will break the present patterns of exploitation by the minority and integrate the dispossessed into the economy as rapidly as possible. Thus far, the patterns of development we have supported have not made much progress toward that goal. As a result, many of those working for development in the Third World simply assume that their choice is between one form or another of socialism. Only as we in America face that fact and work through the implications of it will we be prepared to respond creatively to the challenge presented by the Third World.

During the colonial period, the cards were stacked against the poor peoples of the Third World. The colonial powers used these nations for their own economic advantage. By and large, this is still the case. Private American capital invests abroad because it will make more profits there than at home. We set the prices for the industrial products we sell to them; we also play the dominant role in fixing the prices we pay them for what they sell to us. That was all taken for granted in the past; it no longer is. At a time when our per capita income tends to increase by about two hundred dollars each year, which is more than the total per capita income of many of the underdeveloped countries, that system of economic relationship cannot be tolerated any longer. If our own economy is so powerful, it is time for us to ask ourselves why we should insist on maintaining such a relationship and to begin to explore new possibilities.

American Power

Ultimately, the question raised for us by this situation has to do with our own economic system and the way it operates *at home* as well as abroad. Its development has made it possible for us to arrive at a level of technological advancement and economic production which now challenges the very structures which have produced all this. We have now arrived at a point at which our success in the economic sphere obliges us to raise new questions about our economic goals, about the way our system functions, etc., which are really long overdue. Being confronted by the demands arising out of the Third World, we have the opportunity to participate in a process of transformation which could be of importance for our own economic development as well as for that of the countries of Asia, Africa, and Latin America.

(3) Our concern for the future of our relationships with the Third World must sooner or later focus on the question of our use of military power abroad. For those of us of an older generation who travel abroad with some frequency, the present mood we find almost everywhere shocks us. Accustomed as we have been to thinking of Nazi Germany and later of communist Russia as nations who threatened the peace of the whole world by their irresponsible use of military power, we can hardly adjust to the fact that people everywhere now see the United States in that same role. What is more serious, we are sooner or later forced to the conclusion that their judgment is largely justified. In a world in which many nations on three continents are struggling for changes in their most basic economic, social, and political structures (changes long overdue), we are using our massive military power for containment. As long as we continue to do so, we will be engaged in military operations against revolutionary movements, support torture and repression, and help destroy the best and most committed leaders of a new generation.

What the Religious Revolutionaries Are Saying

Here, as elsewhere, the problem is a complicated one. It is not just a question of getting out of Vietnam as quickly as possible or of taking steps toward cutting military spending. The real issue is that of a change in our consciousness which can lead us to a new understanding of our use of power in the world today and to basic changes in our military goals and strategy. Sooner or later we must come to realize that, in certain circumstances, revolution is the road to peace and stability, and that our own possibilities for the future depend upon our freedom to support those who are creating a new future for the Third World. We may now feel secure if our power contains an explosive situation, and if two or three powerful nations control the world. But it is just possible that in the midst of the chaos and confusion that go with the emergence of new nations, with new ways of life, to a position of participation in international affairs, we will discover new forms of integration, new patterns of peacemaking, and a more interesting and promising world for ourselves as well.

I am not at all sure that the Christian community today can give birth to such small communities of transformation of consciousness. If it should succeed, I do not know how far they will go in providing new models for a desperate world or new power for change in our foreign policy. But I see this as one wager worth making, and I am convinced that, along this path, we will come to new discoveries of the meaning and power of our faith in the present age.

ABOUT THE CITY

JOHN FRY

There has been too much fancy talk glorifying the city, most of it by country boys who are in the first stages of enthusiasm about the privacy and opportunity for creative goofing-off that a city affords. You can do in the city what you want to but cannot do in the country. This verity is then pumped up with romantic gas until the city seems like a wonderful place.

First of all, the city is not a wonderful place, except for the "in" (beautiful) people. The "out" (nonbeautiful) people are glued to the city because they don't have the skills to get the money to move; and by reason of sheer racism many cannot move just anyplace they want to, even if they have the money. Life in the city for the out-people is uncomfortable: pollution is oppressive; services are expensive and difficult to secure; movement is difficult on private or public transportation; the streets are dirty; the few premium entertainment possibilities, such as a great ballet troupe giving a great performance of a great ballet, are set amidst the tedium of mediocre, garish entertainment. There are many personal hazards. The swinging young find impure dope at exaggerated prices and with greater risk than at Scotts Bluff.

What the Religious Revolutionaries Are Saying

These critical descriptive remarks are appropriate for cities as such, not only some cities, such as Chicago and New York. Cities were built by Mammon for the purpose of piling up wealth. Greed is the dominating characteristic of city life. What is necessary for effective greed is untrammeled opportunity and a dense population of people willing to work for next to nothing. By farm standards, wages are fantastically high in the city. That's why so many people migrate to the city. They want those big wages. But the wages only appear to be high. Thus cheap labor is lured to the city by its own greed, only to be overwhelmed by the ultra-privatist assumptions of city life, where no one cares about anyone but himself. Once in the city, the very density, fatigue, suspicion, and hardheartedness of the place tend to produce isolated, pushy laborers. Their struggle with existence itself is so encompassing that they haven't the imagination or energy to contest the assumptions of living in the city at all. What does this mean? The million and one bottom-of-the-ladder jobs in the factories, plants, stores, shops, offices, bureaus, warehouses, terminals, markets, restaurants, theaters, laboratories, buildings, and centers of the city pay ridiculously low wages, which are nevertheless higher than what one can make pumping gas in Galesburg. What does this mean? The owners of the enterprises, the managers of conglomerates of enterprises, the managers of financial institutions owned by—or owning—the congolmerates all get steadily and grossly rich. That is the aim of cities: to sustain a fabulous flow of money out of the hands of the poor into the hands of the rich. It is the essence of irony itself. The rich make their money in part from the cheap labor they gouge and underpay. The laboring force, mostly poor, is "hooked" worse than a strung-out heroin addict because the rich wouldn't have it any other way.

Greed also requires untrammeled opportunity, we said. Yes. That is provided by a political apparatus which uses the many votes of the laboring force, mostly poor, to sustain the wealth-gathering activities of the rich. As a matter of principle, the political apparatus overtaxes and overinspects any property the poor might own while it undertaxes (after underassessing) and underinspects the vast properties of the rich. For such easement of fiscal responsibility to the city treasury, the politicians receive gratuities designed to vault them into power.

The role of policemen is to protect property and keep the cheap laborers so dispirited and bullied that they won't harm private property, run back to the farm, or . . . revolt. Policemen walk a delicate line between showing sufficient force to inspire hopelessness and showing excessive force lest they stir up revolution. Having been at it for decades, they are quite skilled. Their task is made easier by heroin, cheap wine, numbers, and head-crushing fatigue, all of which rob the spirit and inhibit revolution.

We cannot imagine American life without cities. This is a function of increasing urbanization and also, in part, a function of the sheer recollection that life on the farm is not much better either. To say it another way, greed multiplies itself. People who become rich inspire greed in the penurious: they want some, they want a lot. Unless they have talent or inherit a lot of land, they are going to express their greed in the city, not on the farm. So there we are: getting urbanized all over the place—a headlong plunge toward lots of money.

You think I jest. Not so. I am telling the truth about the city. You want statistics perchance, some sociology, some assessments based on evidence? Too bad. The truth about the city is that Mammon built it. Greed is its chief characteristic. It is a miserable place for human beings to live—unless you belong to the "in" crowd. In that case you would be living in opulent splendor, protected by your insulated structure against the misery of your fellow city dwellers. The "in" crowd lives not in the city but in a suburb located inside the city. "In" people do not ride buses, cash their checks at currency exchanges, pay rent in cash, fight rats, get shot at by policemen, get laid off episodically, get cheated in the grocery store, or drive over broken glass in the streets. "In" people move between air-conditioned modules, to work, to fun, to bed, to Puerto Vallerta, to the bank. Misery supports their beautiful lives.

I am not articulating a standard churchly view of the city. My view of the city is heterodox, verging toward heretical. The orthodox view conforms to the view of country boys: the city is where the action is, where it's happening, and other such nonsense. Dismayed by the "irrelevance" of the church to this exciting, stimulating place full of existential psychiatrists, flute players, Stop the War! marches, topless shoe-shine girls, Black Panthers, urban coalitions, the orthodox view is: let's join up. Obviously, the old church thing won't work.

In recent years there have been great heavings in the church. "With-it," "now" Christians have begun saying, "We've got to be imaginative and successful *in the city* or we are going to die because soon it's going to be straight city, from Milwaukee to Boston, from Boston to Miami, from San Diego to San Francisco." I can think of no more pitiful exhibition of ineptitude than the efforts which flowed from all this great heaving and thrashing around. At least the church used to be religious and had *that* to commend itself to an urban populace. But in getting "with it" the church has made a studied attempt to get over these superstitions, this God-talk, this fixation with biblical authority, this antihuman puritan ethics. Plug in the electric guitar! Buy some bell-bottoms! Talk hip! Make religion swing! Since religion manifestly does not swing, the outstanding consequence of trying to get with it is that the church hasn't even got religion to commend it anymore. And it never did have much else. Consider—

First, the church has no more money. Once it did have money and with it did some useful things, like funding "black power." That turned off the conventional flow of money from the wealthy donors because they hate black power. Now that the money is gone how can the church be attractive? It is asking for money. It doesn't give money. Strike one.

Second, the church has no more influence. Once it did have influence because judges, magnates, managers, and other elite people were church members. That influence was dissipated when the church tried to use its clout to produce things like legislation and policy change which were *rightly* perceived by the elite to be against their self-interest. Therefore, the church's influence has diminished almost to zero. It cannot phone around, use names, and get useful things like jobs, a ticket fixed, an apartment, a loan, a recommendation. So, how can the church be attractive and important? It doesn't have influence; it is seeking influence. Strike two.

Third, the church has no power. Once it did have power. It could sway elections, for instance. But the old members have died off so fast, and the young have such a studied contempt for the church, that it cannot use its members, wealth, or influence to *hurt* someone—which is the nature of power. So, how can the church be attractive as a real power force? It doesn't have power; it desires power. Strike three. And out.

We are certainly not talking about radical change or minuscule change. The church has been pressing onward toward the high goal of playing the urban game, just trying to get the feel of the city. It hasn't had time to do much aside from the prepossessing task of being relevant.

The recent church experience of disastrous failure is scarcely lamentable. I view it as a work of divine humor. The church has had no better luck moving into the action than poor people have, or black people have, or Chicago people have. They have been making their push, too. They have organized. They have rushed down to city hall. They have actuated the mechanisms guaranteed to produce a citizen voice in public policy. And they have failed. They have no more money, power, influence, or hope of getting them than when they started. The city, characterized by greed, can also be spelled WHITE POWER. Mammon was a white man.

By a work of what I view to be divine humor a church chastened of power-reaching illusions has the present opportunity to see itself as it really is: powerless and as poor as the black poor. Because it is so stuffy and has aristocratic memories, this is a hard picture of itself to endure, but it is a real picture. If the truth saves, then that's the picture to look at: the church as nigger.

The soteriological offshoots of the picture are varied and numerous. Such as:

(1) The church can recognize real substantial enemies, namely, the power people. These people were assiduously courted during the relevance psychosis—I mean politicians, policemen, bankers, rich people, magnates, and the like. All the time they were enemies. They are now recognized as enemies. They are responsible for human wreckage. Their hegemony must therefore be challenged, or, failing that, at least despised.

(2) The church can participate actively in the widespread and growing urban misery. The city is not swinging discotheques, it is people dying while traveling from a private hospital which will not let them into its emergency room to a public hospital which has to. The city is Harlem, not Central Park East, West, or South. I do not mean that the church can stand in the midst of the misery with millions of dollars or words of hope. The church stands there as miserable as anybody else, yelling about what the city does to poor people.

(3) The church can begin to feel the pain of impossible polarization. Black anger over the arrogance of white racism only hardens the racism, which doubles black anger.

The City

And so on. Thus to the ordinary perils of city life have been added lately the additional risks of violence aimed at one's race, not one's particular person. These violent possibilities exist because people have a superstitious belief in the efficacy of retribution. Black people feel good about getting even. White people feel good about their policemen smashing down this black revolt. Nobody gets even. Everybody's public safety is further degraded. What are the answers? The church can lead the way in establishing that there are no answers. There is no way out of the impossible polarization—short of abolishing racism itself, which is too close to greed for us to consider as a historical possibility, although it may be constructed as an eschatological possibility.

(4) The church can begin to transmute its longings for civil peace, green grass, clean water, and clean air into visions of a traumatically deurbanized America. Greed requires human sacrifices that simply are too great and that must no longer be served as a *prima facie* good. The slums of the country do not want rebuilding, they want destruction, and, with it, the destruction of the assumptions which built them in the first place. It is a contradiction in terms to say *great cities* meaning thereby merely big. The dismantling of the biggest cities means the dismantling of the fantastically easy way the rich have gotten their money. It means dismantling the welfare racket. It means dismantling the public transportation system. It means dismantling the very axes of political power in this country. It means a slowly *shrinking* gross national product.

I find it strange that anyone would talk about the "greening of America" when so much of it is already green: waiting to be lived on and played on. The drastic change—on the order of a truly wild revolution—to be contemplated is not the reordering of power in cities but the dismantling of the cities themselves. The hordes of city dwellers who have recently fled to suburbs had half a good idea. They did not flee far enough; they fled from what they saw as the problem, namely, colored people. So they did not flee greed, but keep coming back into the city every workday to pick up some gold. The impulse to move away, however, is sound, human, and revolutionary. It is hardly traditional to consider the subtly racist, timid suburbanite a revolutionary harbinger. But he is. He found city life intolerable and acted intelligently and radically.

A poor, powerless church—chastened of relevance illusions—is without money, influence, and power in the city. The church learns something from poor people by itself being poor; the church learns something from powerless people by itself being powerless. What it learns is to recognize this life as the life of the mighty king Jesus, hence the church's appropriate life. Finally, after many centuries of dabbling in aristocratic zones—and if Max Weber is right, after practically inventing middle-class white power ethics—the church has been put down to its true position, at least in the city. Out in the suburbs it still has pretensions, class, money, and uses its influence and power to shore up the decadent-revolutionary suburban structure. But the church is right down there in the dirty city streets with the poor and unemployed.

The church hasn't known what it means *not* to succeed. In America, the church has always succeeded. It has always grown. Its budgets have always gone up. Its buildings have been torn down in order to build new and bigger ones. Its membership lists have always expanded. Only in the last twelve years has the church had to face decline, rebuff, unsuccess. As we have noted, the unsuccess is not remarkable in the suburbs and other zones of white power land. But it is remarkable, astounding, in the city. We cannot fortuitously assume that unsuccess is failure, however. Unsuccess is to be reckoned ouside the success-failure scale. Any ragged ten-year-old boy standing on his slum stoop knows that much theology. Unsuccess is a mode of being outside an entire world determining itself along the success-failure scale. Unsuccess thus comprehensively states a range of hopes not reckoned along that scale. These happen to be human hopes, anchored in the gross need to survive. Around that need hope regards cheer, ease from hunger, ease from fatigue, ease from summary violence as indisputable goods. The church as *unsuccessful* comes back home to be there in that mode. Not to hope for success, then, does not describe the reality of hopelessness. It describes hope among the indigenously hopeful, a hope not designed toward money or inspired by greed.

What has this preacher of a manifestly unsuccessful church in the wretchedly greedy city of Chicago got to say about the prospects of deurbanization? What are my credentials for evaluating the prospects for a reordering of political power? They are slim. I am not among the powerful and the successful who must struggle with these mighty possibilities. I do not belong to those who have fled the city, whose decadent-revolutionary actions may yet actuate the dismantling of cities. I dwell, rather, among the lumpen-lumpen, the truly déclassés, who have to dig out a place to stand—and to live—in a hostile, death-bound environment.

The archaisms of apostolic preaching and of prophetic discernment become the only offices available to the church in the city.

It is not the function of the church to comment on spectacular (world-historical) issues, trends, currents, possibilities, as though the comment were important, or that people were eager to be advised by the comment. It is rather the function of the church to treasure its impactlessness, its insignificance as its insignia. Apostolic preaching and prophetic discernment, you will note, are not directed toward the city desk, the TV talk-show, or the mayor. They are directed toward God's people. Although the archaisms of preaching and prophesying seem ludicrously impotent in the power-force field of a city, they are nonetheless the authentic churchly offices. They are well fitted for the mode of being unsuccessful. They are merely the means of God's meeting with his people in judgment and grace. Put another way, they are merely independent address and, perforce, almost the only freely spoken words to be heard in the city. They are the obverse of greed, the enemy of slums, the challenge to repression, and a source of inspiration among human beings.

We are so accustomed to judging functions on the basis of usefulness that we now want to reassign significance to preaching and prophesying within the success-failure scale. After all, "freely spoken words" have an obvious political content; and on that line of reasoning, "freely spoken words" are also revolutionary words. I want to rebut that imputed significance. Preaching and prophesying do not arouse revolution or impede revolution. They upbuild the soul, they inspire the spirit, they *new* the new mind which we have in Christ Jesus, as an archaic apostolic preacher put it (Rom. 12:1-2). Therefore, they are eligible for suspicion and potentially brutal reprisal from the police force.

When *the church* is thrown against the wall as a common criminal, as a junkie, as a political pariah, it is assumed that the church has become too "hot" politically. This is normally (and erroneously) assumed. Not so. The church gets busted for not having enough political concern, for doing and saying things which are apolitical. "Freely spoken words" in the unsuccess mode tend to be heard by "freely acting people" whose actions are novel and incalculably unpredictable; but they are perceived to be threatening and communist by city hall. The story of Herod killing all boy babies in order to cut down his rival Jesus has a natural reference to the church in the city. Who could see in a powerless, poor, miserable bunch of déclassés a political threat? Police can. That's who. And they will persist in busting the church as long as the church freely says and

The City

freely does. The labor force is being tampered with, you know. The market for heroin and loans to be repaid at twenty-five percent interest is getting uppity, you know. The people are calling the mayor a despot, you know. Why, only last week I saw a graffitum which read, "Off the Pharisees!" Too much. So, up against the wall, you MFS.

Perhaps someday there will be no more city in America. I think the preconditions for that possibility are:

(1) The abolition of racism.
(2) The abolition of poverty and poverty's normative slum environment.
(3) The abolition of centralized (and centralizing) political power.
(4) The abolition of centralized (and centralizing) industrial power.

The actualization of these preconditions is well within the nation's technological and moral competence. Greed alone stands in the way. It is nonsense for the church immodestly to assign to itself the task of smashing down greed. Rather, the church has been slammed up against the wall by the agencies of Greed. I suspect the more the church proceeds flat-outward in its preaching and prophesying, the closer America comes to the preconditions for deurbanization. I did not, however, learn this from the Lord. It is my guess. It is the thoroughly happy guess of a man who has fought city hall and lost so many times that he can cheerfully want to see city hall made into a museum to which school children will one day come in much the same spirit of amazement as school children presently visiting Belsen, Treblinka, Dachau, and Auschwitz.

BLACK POWER
IN THE CHURCH

JAMES E. WOODRUFF

Revolution is a word of many different meanings. To young militants and activists it is a serious commitment to the destruction of the present system of government. To others it is something that occurred in the past, ushering in a new government to correct the mistakes of the old. We are now in the astrological "Age of Aquarius," during which time revolution is supposed to flourish.

Despite the many meanings that characterize this word revolution, it is clear that they all mean *change*. Furthermore, they mean change from an unsatisfactory government to one that is hopefully better. To this end, theology must speak emphatically about the ultimate meaning of revolution. Theology would be hard pressed to find a more relevant task than to be involved in revolution.

Yet there are religionists who are convinced that revolution should not be the concern of God's people. Perhaps this is because they do not understand the basic truth captured in the concept of revolution. Perhaps these people are not yet aware of the fact that they have been programmed, been taught to believe that the present governmental situation is indeed the best for all possible worlds. As a consequence of this kind of thinking, they view any desire or attempt to change this order as anarchistic and unjustified, a violent assault to be put down and punished.

Black Power in the Church

The meaning of the concept of revolution is ambiguous because there is an important sense in which change is always going on. Change is usually normal and continuous, but it can be rapid and violent. Sometimes actual change is so slow that it is virtually imperceptible. Although revolution is usually associated with violent change, this is not always the case. The Industrial Revolution is an example of slow and steady change. Admittedly, the American Industrial Revolution was the main factor leading to the Civil War, which was by no means slow or imperceptible. Nevertheless, words such as evolution, change, and innovation, when used in a political sense, are all part of the essential meaning of the word *revolution* in that they all aid man in creating an order in which he can survive.

Governments change through revolution, innovation, and evolution; the fact is that they must change. The role and function of government is to divide the power in a way that will satisfy the governed. When this is done effectively, there will be peace. The job, then, of the active political process is to divide the power in ways acceptable to the citizenry. However, the special meaning of the concept of revolution is that when the division of power is unjust or unbalanced, the dissatisfaction of the powerless will cause an attempt to force a new distribution of power. Sometimes this is done through the use of arms, while at other times the strike or the boycott might achieve the intended goals.

The particular problem of the contemporary American revolution is first to clarify the way that power is actually distributed in America. Once this is done, if the conclusion indicates that a change is necessary which cannot wait for the normal legislative process, then what? The church must speak to both aspects of this problem.

Power in the United States is shared by three groups: white Protestants, white Catholics, and white Jews. These three groups control the financial, educational, judicial, and social institutions in the United States. If there is any debate over the accuracy of that observation, there surely can be no argument about the conclusion to which this assertion leads, namely, that black Americans have no share of the legitimate power in this country. Black representation in the control of any of the above-mentioned institutions is negligible. Therefore, the first conclusion is that the present distribution of power is totally unacceptable to one tenth of the citizens of the United States. This is not to say that only black people are dissatisfied; this is one clear and important example of political dissatisfaction.

The political dissatisfaction of black Americans arises not only from the fact that black people are clearly oppressed but, more importantly, from the fact that there is really no desire on the part of the government to change this untenable reality. Since the founding of this nation there has been a clear, consistent, and successful attempt to strip non-whites of any potential power. The means used were slave-masters and their armies of overseers and slave hunters, Southern sheriffs, bloodhounds, and the gigantic lie that black people were not as human as white people. After the Civil War, Jim Crowism, segregation laws, lynchings, mob violence, and all-white legislation and jurors were among the primary tools used. In modern times, the main difference is that to the list must now be added the riot-trained police and national guard, technology, and immigration laws. All of this, in short, points vividly to tyrannical governments strengthened by customs and mores that are so widely accepted that the second question of revolution is not as easily answered as the first.

The deplorable condition of black people coupled with the fact that there has been, up to now, no serious effort to change the reality of an unjust social and political order, means that the conditions that breed revolution are present.

It is to this reality that American revolutionaries have developed their strategies. At this stage there are many. The black caucus of the Episcopal church has been involved in a revolutionary attempt to change the decision-making apparatus of this white, wealth-dominated denomination. This caucus is officially called the Union of Black Clergy and Laity of the Episcopal Church, and is fondly referred to by its members as "the Union." The goals of the Union are as follows:

(1) To eradicate racism from within the Episcopal church, whereby the church can overcome its division and paralysis.

(2) To protect and minister to the needs of each other as brothers, whereby we can establish "the equality and humanity of every child of God, removing the malevolent welfare and financial insecurity from both clergy and lay Episcopalians."

(3) To demonstrate the crucial importance of a stronger black voice in the determination of policy and the implementing of programs within both the diocesan and national setting particularly as they pertain to urban affairs. An authentic and proper position of leadership for black parishes.

(4) To provide an instrument for determining the consensus of black opinion within the Episcopal church and community concerning crucial issues facing the church.

(5) To assist black parishes with the development of more authentic liturgical expression of black style and experience, and to create a relevant program of urban Christian education.

(6) To provide a resource bank of skilled black churchmen to aid in the development of effective programs in problematic areas on a parochial, diocesan, or national level.

(7) To help create opportunities for authentic interdependent mission cooperation between white suburban parishes and their urban counterpart.

The initial strategy of the Union was to echo the note sounded by the "Black Manifesto." This essentially meant that the Union's first task was to clarify categorically the racist posture of the Episcopal church. Episcopalians were confronted with the reality that their church has always been run by and in the interest of its white members.

The Union surfaced clearly at a special general convention of the Episcopal church held in South Bend, Indiana, on the campus of the University of Notre Dame in September 1969. Although the Union gave its principal energy to influencing this national church body to give money to the Black Economic Development Corporation, a larger victory was won. The composition of the Executive Council of the church was changed to include six minority representatives, two of whom were appointed by the Union. For the first time in the history of this church's participation in Christianity there were members of this highest council who were not elected. It was a clear admission of the church's racism.

However, what we were to learn was that merely to admit or confess racism is not enough. Racism is not merely a state of mind that exists, but instead is a way of life that is perpetrated by force. This particular way of life is demonstrated vividly in the obvious inequality displayed in the division of power in our society. Unfortunately, this is what a social evaluation of the race problem would suggest. The general conclusion of most social analyses is that black and white people dislike or hate each other; therefore, they conclude, the answer is to start treating each other kindly. The mistake here is that no attention is paid to the real causes. If the solution is that love is what is needed then we should be able to conclude that it was the lack of love that brought the problem about. However, the cause of the problem was not a lack of love but the presence of identifiable color which made it easy ruthlessly to control black people. There can be no escape when your skin is your uniform, the permanent badge of slavery in America.

The question of whether the black caucus of the Episcopal church is an effective revolutionary effort will be determined by the results. If our caucus can morally persuade our church to divest itself of its unjustly gained resources, then we will have performed a revolutionary act without raising a gun.

Black Power in the Church

Our faith in our ability to persuade the church morally is based on two factors. The first is that we are offering viable alternatives which are attractive in themselves. The second is that we believe that white churchmen can readily see that the hour is late. This society needs leadership on how to stop being racist. If we can force a white racist church to bend to black control, perhaps this can indeed be a Christian revolution which is perhaps what Ezekiel was prophesying when he saw "a wheel in the middle of a wheel."

THE
POLICE PROBLEM

DAVID M. GRACIE

"Police forces now form a virtually independent sub-
culture that is less and less responsive to the civilian
population that they are supposed to protect." (Harvey
Cox)

The nub of the police problem in our cities today has to
do with responsiveness and accountability. Whose police
are they? Whom do they serve? How can I hold them accountable when they mistreat me or fail to prevent crime
in my community?

I would like to encourage you to try to look at the police
through the eyes of the black community and then ask
those questions. Next, look at the police through the eyes
of those who are organizing to bring about change in our
society, including those in the emerging youth culture
whose style of life represents a threat to traditional
values.

To acknowledge that there is a "police problem" is not to
deny that there is a growing problem of crime or that
policemen often risk and sometimes lose their lives. To
deny that there is a "police problem," however, may be to
ignore one of the most serious threats to our society. For
many readers this will be an exercise in empathy, a neces-

sary one, I think, and one that should extend, in conclusion, to the plight of the policeman himself.

Police and the Black Community

"There was open warfare between Detroit Negroes and the Detroit Police Department." Thus Judge George Edwards described the 1943 Detroit race riot.[1] That open warfare, which has flared up again in the years since 1964, is the outgrowth of a continuing conflict between black communities everywhere and the police. Its day-to-day expression is police brutality.

"Here came this cop with no shirt on, with a judo lock around the neck of this fellow, a colored man, and he was shouting, 'You big black mother- ———, you come on now, come on, get in here.' He couldn't move him, so he took two handcuffs and put them around his hand and hit him on the forehead and just split his head open." So reported the assistant of United States Congressman John Conyers concerning what he had seen at a police station in the summer of 1967.[2]

It was not until the recent rebellions that many white people came to believe that police brutality was real. The Kerner Report, John Hersey's *Algiers Motel Incident,* and other studies made it plain enough. Some police were capable of anything, including cold-blooded murder.

It is important to recognize that "police brutality" does not just mean splitting a man's head open or other physical abuse; it means also the humiliation, harassment, and verbal abuse directed by the police against citizens. A survey of south central Los Angeles residents, taken by the University of California at Los Angeles, revealed that 45 percent of the people had witnessed police brutality, defined as physical abuse, while 80 percent claimed that the police used insulting language in the ghetto.[3] The latter

41

figure is the most significant because it reveals why the police are almost universally regarded as a hostile, alien force in the ghetto.

The Kerner Report showed that the first grievance of ghetto residents across the land had to do with police practices.[4] There can be no question that the alienation of the black community from the police is almost complete.

The attitudes of the police toward the black community are starkly revealed by Professor Alfred Reiss's study in a large city: "In predominantly Negro precincts, over three-fourths of the white policemen express prejudiced attitudes toward Negroes. Only one percent of the officers expressed attitudes which could be described as sympathetic toward Negroes. Indeed, close to one-half of all the police officers in predominantly Negro high crime areas showed extreme prejudice against Negroes. What do I mean by extreme racial prejudice? I mean that they describe Negroes in terms that are not people terms. They describe them in terms of the animal kingdom."[5]

I believe that the social analysis which is best capable of dealing with this history of warfare and this set of extreme attitudes is one which understands the ghetto as a colony. We are dealing with a colonial situation, with the police operating not only to patrol and control the ghetto, but also to dehumanize the colonized people who reside there. The intense feelings and acts generated in response to this brutalization are those of an oppressed people who want to be free. Officer Paille's description of the mood of black people on the streets during the Detroit rebellion is revealing: "I noticed these people on the side, they all had smiles on their faces and everything else, just like they had just accomplished something. I couldn't understand that, and I asked one fellow, 'What's wrong with you people?' And he said, 'If you think you've got it now, just wait until later on; we're really going to get you fellows.' . . . So this was the general impression I got from these people: They didn't want any help or nothing, all they wanted to do was take over themselves."[6]

That was, in fact, what they wanted! The Kerner Report and other studies of the rebellions have revealed the demand for self-determination and control of social and political institutions by the black people who rebelled.

It is therefore possible to describe the police in the ghettos as an army of occupation, a force that must be withdrawn—through defeat or grant of power—before the police problem can be solved. The Black Panthers are saying this today, but a couple of years ago it was being said by someone who is no Black Panther.

Dr. Arthur Niederhoffer of the City College of New York, a former policeman and the author of *Behind the Shield,* gave a thorough analysis of the police as an occupying army in a speech delivered in Philadelphia in 1968. He compared the police to the United States Army in Vietnam: the army is white and white supremacist, while the occupied citizens are people of color; the army tends to escalate the conflict by introducing newer, more sophisticated weapons; its tactics are aggressive patrol and counterinsurgency; its avowed goals, however, are pacification and the building up of responsibility and self-help in the community; there is lack of communication between the army and the population; there are doves and hawks on both sides; the army claims to be bringing law and order but the residents say they bring repression, brutality, and even death.

Proposed solutions to the police problem that fail to see the crisis in its true proportions are no solutions. The Kerner Report is a good example of this tunnel vision approach. The usual set of reforms are recommended (and some of them on the surface sound good), but the colonial context is not dealt with. The supplement to the Report, on "Control of Disorder," is the giveaway. The police are to continue to be an occupation force, albeit a more humane and efficient one. Police intelligence units are encouraged to spy on the community. Chemical weapons are to be used instead of bullets, but we have plenty of evidence now that tear gas and MACE can be used for the same repressive, dehumanizing purposes as billy clubs and shotgun shells.

The usual reforms include professionalization of the police. We need a new breed, says William W. Turner in his book *The Police Establishment*. He proposes that men like Chief Headley of Miami who "declared war" on the Negro area be replaced by men like San Francisco's Lt. Dante Andreotti, whose community relations program was widely acclaimed. He does not note, or perhaps he did not know, that Andreotti's great program was too good for the system to tolerate.[7] Turner does not sense that a racist power structure *wants* men like Headley in command of the police.

Whole sets of reforms—like higher recruitment standards, more education and training, civilian review boards, community service officers (junior policemen), more black police, guidelines on the use of weapons—can be of small value in themselves if they do not address the basic question, which is one of *power*. Who controls the police? To whom are they responsible—the white power structure or the black community? There is evidence to show the lack of importance of reform measures. "If the 1964 rioting is indicative and if a 1966 survey by the University of California School of Criminology is reliable, the Philadelphia review board has not soothed the Negroes' resentment of the police or restored their confidence in complaint procedures," says Dr. Fogelson.[8] And, of course, the review board is no longer allowed to function, whatever its former worth. But further research is not needed to show the hollow nature of many proposed reforms. The Kerner Commission called for guidelines on the use of police weapons. Who was to prepare the guidelines? The mayors. Mayor Daley did: "Shoot to kill arsonists; shoot to maim looters."

The Police Problem

Police and Those Who Press for Change

Events at the 1968 Chicago convention of the Democratic party, documented in the Walker Report,[9] have revealed to any who doubted that the police are not just the black man's problem but everyone's problem. They are especially the problem of everyone who moves for serious social change. Dormant memories of the role of the police as strikebreakers come alive again. Parallels with Nazi Germany are drawn and accepted by increasing numbers of white people.

A newspaper account of an exchange between Philadelphia CORE director Bill Mathis and a state trooper is illuminating. They were discussing Mayor Daley's dictum that arsonists and looters should be shot. "Isn't he really saying, 'Don't loot or burn or break the law and you won't be harmed?'" asked the trooper. Mathis responded, "What he is saying is: 'Accept the conditions of life I force on you or I will kill you.'"

Police will be used to deal harshly with any group which refuses to accept present social conditions. In this regard, police perform the same function in the white community as in the black: to protect the "power structure," which has a vested economic interest in the status quo, from people who demand self-determination, i.e., the ability to make the decisions that affect their own lives.

But policemen are not simply pawns on a chessboard, who can be coldly placed in position to protect an induction center against peace demonstrators or a high school against student organizers. They bring with them into these encounters attitudes and emotions which can spark violence. Dr. Spiegel of the Lemberg Center for the Study of Violence has written: "To the Irish, Italian or Polish police officer of working class background, black-skinned activists and youthful protesters are the embodiment of everything that is alien, evil and destructive of the American social system. Militant youths and black militants are perceived not only as un-American, but also as non-human. Ruled out of the human race, they become nonpersons and therefore deserving of intense attack, as one would attack a rattlesnake."[10]

On the other side, and in response to the way in which police are used to suppress dissent and the new youth culture, the police come to be viewed as subhuman. I am afraid that empathy will not carry many people to an understanding of this. The "unpoor, uncolored, and unyoung" have a hard time understanding anyone calling a policeman a pig. But, for a starter, go and see Antonioni's film *Zabriskie Point*. This motion picture provides an emotional and aesthetic sense of how the police culture and the youth culture exist in basic opposition: regimented vs. spontaneous, punitive vs. accepting, closed vs. open. The conflict between the two is so explicit in this film that I believe any viewer who has eyes to see will be looking at events differently after he leaves the theater.

Hersey and Antonioni show that the artist's eye is needed fully to perceive this conflict. The eye of the Christian, accustomed to following the Stations of the Cross, should also be able to see. Jesus stands before Pilate, the threatening new culture before the powerful old; spontaneous love before official pigishness; the ethnic rebel before the white colonial ruler. The law enforcement agents deal with Jesus by means of brutality, a rigged trial, and an official execution. They deal with his followers by attempting to divide and terrorize them.

This is the story of Jesus and the authoritarian power structure. Only when we are ready to follow him by sharing his suffering at the hands of official violence can we hear or speak his words of forgiveness that extend even to brutal police, judges, and executioners. Anything short of that is based on sentimentality, not faith in the just God who takes the side of the oppressed.

The Policeman's Problem

It would be utterly unfair to view police officers, both white and black, as anything other than victims of a system gone bad. The police have to be made accountable, not only for the sake of the communities they serve but for their own sake. As long as they are trapped in a police institution which is authoritarian and is used in inhuman ways, they themselves will be dehumanized. Consider the statement of James W. Smith, a former California highway patrol officer: "I was assigned to the Watts area and I found myself roughing up Negroes routinely in the back seat of the patrol car—not because I disliked Negroes, but because in the police group it was the thing to do."[11]

We have required the police to become the dirty-workers of a racially oppressive system and at the same time we have allowed them to suffer from an exploitative economic system, with mortgages and the wartime cost of living on their backs. "You must consider," said one college-educated patrolman, "that many cops have just bought houses in Farmingdale, Long Island, that many are in the process of escaping from boyhoods in the white slums and that this tends to make them super-middle-class."[12]

We tell the police to be enforcers of white, middle-class morality and then frustrate them in doing it. (They perceive liberal rulings from the Supreme Court as frustrations.) We encourage them to make a career of police work and then frustrate them with low salaries and poor chances for advancement and education. Cops have problems. They have a very high suicide rate. Will we deliver them to the Harringtons of the Fraternal Order of Police and the Birch Society so that their racism can be sharpened and their middle-class frustrations used to make good Nazis of them all? Are there any alternatives for the policeman?

I think that any gain in the direction of making the police system accountable and responsive to the community provides an alternative for the policemen themselves. Our goal should be a police force in which police can function as respected servants of the community, rewarded for effective work and held strictly accountable to the community for misconduct or inefficiency. This force should have a high tolerance for social change, even a desire for it, based on their understanding of the people's needs.

In the midst of present divisions, it is important to preserve a vision of a free society, in which cries of "Power to the People" would not be coupled with chants of "Off the Pig."

NOTES

1. *Report of the National Advisory Commission on Civil Disorders* ("Kerner Report") (New York: Bantam Books, 1968), p. 85.

2. John Hersey, *The Algiers Motel Incident* (New York: Alfred Knopf, 1968), pp. 31-32.

3. Study by Walter J. Raine, cited in Fogelson, "From Resentment to Confrontation," *Political Science Quarterly,* June 1968.

4. *Report on Civil Disorders,* Summary, p. 7.

5. Ibid., p. 307.

6. Hersey, *Algiers Motel Incident,* p. 96.

7. See *Fortune,* January 1968, p. 195.

8. "From Resentment to Confrontation," p. 242.

9. *Rights in Conflict: The Walker Report to the National Commission on the Causes and Prevention of Violence* (New York: Bantam Books, 1969).

10. Quoted in "Police Violence: A Changing Pattern," *New York Times,* July 7, 1968.

11. William Turner, *The Police Establishment* (New York: Putnam, 1968).

12. Quoted in "Police Violence: A Changing Pattern."

RECOMMENDED READING

In addition to the works listed above or referred to in the body of the essay, two recent studies are well worth obtaining: Paul Chevigny, *Police Power: Police Abuses in New York City* (New York: Random House, 1969); and W. H. Ferry, "Our Cities: Police States?" *Fellowship Magazine,* January 1970.

The Police Problem

*Council of Organizations on Philadelphia Police
Accountability and Responsibility (COPPAR)*

(The following is a "position paper" prepared in March of 1970 by a Philadelphia coalition from the black, Spanish-speaking, and social activist communities. This paper, included here as illustrative material, serves both to underscore the argument of the preceding essay concerning police accountability and to indicate what actions citizens may take.)

There are two issues which require the immediate attention of this group:

1. *Lack of Police Accountability:* The basic premise that must be comprehended is that the present mode of police conduct exists only because there is a solid majority of support in our City for such behavior. This majority has been persuaded, or believes out of its fears, that minimal restraints should be placed on the police because otherwise the "criminal elements" will overrun the community. A portion of the majority even recognizes that the police have a tendency to abuse some of the people they deal with. But, their reasoning goes, this is an unfortunate but acceptable necessity in the fight against crime.

The fallacy of the majority view is that few of the abuses committed by the police are directed against either organized crime or professional criminals. It is the general experience of such criminals that they suffer little, if any, substantial personal harassment at the hands of the police. But, all citizens, whether or not they have committed any unlawful acts, are entitled to be free from mistreatment of any kind at the hands of the police. Police abuses largely arise from the relations between the police and the socially discontented elements of our City—the poor, the blacks, the Spanish-speaking and the young. These are the groups that the majority is frustrated by; frustrated because they insistently refuse to accept the role of being an "under class" in our City.

It is the misuse of the police by the majority for the purpose of trying to control discontent, rather than crime, which produces abuses of power by the police.

A police department which is fully accountable to the community for its actions is not inconsistent with good law enforcement. On the contrary, police misbehavior generates hostility and community alienation which in turn generates an atmosphere of disregard for law.

The first step in establishing police accountability for the use of power is to make a substantial portion of the community

What the Religious Revolutionaries Are Saying

aware that such conduct (a) is not fundamentally directed against organized crime and professional criminals, (b) has no relevance to the attempts to control street crime and (c) that it is succeeding in splitting the City into hostile and dangerous camps.

The second step in establishing police accountability is to devise mechanisms for making the police responsible to civilian control, without interfering with its crime fighting ability.

2. *Police Political Coercion:* The "hands-off the police" attitude that now grips the majority of the City has produced a new and dangerous phenomenon; that is, the police as an open and active instrument of political coercion. Within the past year we have witnessed a number of notorious acts of political coercion by the police, for example:

(a) Untrue and malicious attacks on the United Fund for allegedly supporting legal activities of which the police disapproved;

(b) Pressure on the City Government to harass and punish employees who are critical of police misconduct;

(c) Coercion of Judges to return verdicts and impose sentences in line with police rather than judicial standards;

(d) The attempted take over of the Private Defender Agency by the City which among other things would tend to prevent it from being an effective means for the poor to fight police abuses;

(e) The enactment of ordinances, at the insistence of the police, to permit the entry of police onto college and school campuses to conduct searches;

(f) The appointment of two ranking police officials to positions in civilian departments of the City Government;

(g) Political threats by the police against a Councilman as a result of criticism by his wife of the two police appointments referred to above;

(h) Threats against lawyers for bringing suit for the removal of policemen involved in repeated abuses of citizens;

(i) The groundwork being laid for a compaign to make Police Commissioner Frank Rizzo Mayor of Philadelphia.

The purposes of this organization (COPPAR) are three-fold: educational, political and direct action.

Educational: There are two principal reasons for pursuing this function. First, the majority that now accepts police abuse of power cannot be moved away from this position until the facts are made known to them of the extent and the objects of police mistreatment. This information is not now available through any source, including the police department, even if it were willing to

The Police Problem

release information. COPPAR will perform the totally unique function of ferreting out, gathering and disseminating the facts on police abuses to a wide audience.

Second, there exists a substantial imbalance in the reporting of the mass media on the problems of police and crime. There is more than adequate coverage of the various criminal offenses committed daily. However, the daily newspapers and the major radio and television outlets on the whole ignore the police problem. This is partly because they rely upon the police for much of the information they print about crimes and because they believe that meaningful criticism of the police initiated by the media will make their job of gathering crime news from the police more difficult. COPPAR believes it can fill the gap and become a major news source for the media on the police problem.

Political: It is imperative that action be taken now to give the people of Philadelphia meaningful control over the conduct of the police. To achieve this, there must be a restructuring of the City Government. COPPAR will seek to rally organizations and citizens to create sufficient political effectiveness to achieve these changes.

Direct Action: Many persons oppressed by the police are unaware of how and where they may be able to obtain legal redress for police abuses. When COPPAR receives complaints for which there may be redress, it will seek to bring aggrieved persons together with individuals and organizations who can provide appropriate help. COPPAR will also seek to unite organizations and individuals to publicly protest both departmental and individual abuses of power on the part of police.

THE JEWISH
COMMUNITY—WHERE IT'S AT

ARTHUR GILBERT

The secular press has not yet given adequate attention to a significant revolution now taking place within the Jewish community. Granted, Judaism has no pope, no requirement of celibacy for the religious, no Father Berrigan. There is no rabbi of Billy Graham's stature, no World Council of Churches against whom South Africa can rail. The reactionary Jewish Defense League hardly matches Carl McIntire in press-appeal and Black Power groups rarely organize campaigns for reparations within the Jewish community. Thus, few Americans are aware of the radical religious action within the Jewish community today. This is unfortunate, for what is happening inside our community is a portent of things to come. Jews have frequently been the "bellwether" people of Western civilization. A description of the Jewish community today offers a clue to the direction in which other religious groups may move in the near future. It suggests those changes that all religions will have to make if they wish to have the loyalty of the "now generation."

Regrettably, however, anti-Semitism is still a fact of life. This explains both Jewish weakness and Jewish strength. It accounts for the inability, or unwillingness, of Christian scholars to pierce the surface of our communal life; but it also explains why Jews are reluctant to disclose the truth of our crisis. It shows why questions of physical survival still take precedence for Jews over proposals for interior radical change. A radical's approach to religious issues seems a luxury for a threatened Jewish people.

Mordecai M. Kaplan, as early as 1935, rejected a personal, supernaturalist God and offered instead a concept of God as process. But this fact was lost to the world of philosophy in the wake of Auschwitz and the drama of Israel's emergence. Decades later, Bonhoeffer, Robinson, Pike, Hamilton, Altizer, et al., stirred the intellectual world with concepts no more revolutionary than those *earlier* propounded by Kaplan.[1]

Jews, in any event, have their own reasons for reassessing traditional theological tenets. Not only did they endure, later than other religious groups, the baptism of emancipation and an unsettling confrontation with science, but in the fires of the holocaust they experienced God's apparent impotence in a most horrifying and soul-searing way, and have not yet recovered from that trauma. Our traditional liturgies today meet with more resistance than ever before. Jews attend religious worship services less frequently than members of any other American religious group. Jewish intellectuals abandon their religion more decisively than do Protestants or Catholics.

On the other hand, Jews consider themselves not a church but a *people*. One becomes Jewish by attachment to that people—no matter how tenuous the connection may be, or whether it is by affirmative conviction or Christian coercion. Religious commitment or belief is only one aspect of being Jewish. Jews have long established institutions beyond synagogal control for defensive social action, philanthropy, and education. Well before Harvey Cox's provocative call to Christians to minister to the secular world, Jews were out in the world, an urbanized and secularized people. Indeed, some Jews are now becoming disillusioned with the secular and with universalism. The aloneness we endured in Nazi Germany, the silence we hear as Israel struggles for life, the inner hollowness we know to be the consequence of a compulsively successful pursuit of material security have caused many Jews to turn back to the richness of their traditions and particularity. Stimulated by the search of Black Americans for a heritage, we have rediscovered with joy our own vital and meaningful, if painful, history. But it is a history that desperately needs reconstruction and updating. Thus many Jews who find their religion antiquated still take pride in the heritage of Jewish history and heroism.

The Jews have never separated sexuality from their humanity; celibacy and virginity are not considered higher states of being. We know how dangerous the puritanical repression of the sexual instincts is, but we have been unable to protect ourselves completely from the effects of the hypocrisy and sickness fostered by Western culture. Now that the power of those mores has been weakened, Jews are flocking unashamedly to a "new morality." Happily, that morality still requires that the whole self be bound to the flesh in the celebration of life's greatest joy, not as a fulfillment of a supernatural Torah law but rather as a self-evident spiritual truth of profound human significance. They are seeking more authentic interpersonal sexual relations.[2]

We know a tyrant when we see one, for the Jews have been sensitized by generations of persecution. We opposed Senator Joseph McCarthy long before America caught on; today we distrust Vice-President Spiro Agnew in far greater numbers than others. The *New York Times,* October 11, 1970, reported that 22 percent of Catholics thought Agnew "harmful," 39 percent of Protestants and 69 percent of Jews. We are concerned that America's democratic process will not withstand the stress of polarization. Many of us are considered to be "radical liberals." Of course, this frightens some Jews almost to death, for the soil in a rightist "Amerika" will be ripe for the ugly weed of a disastrous Jew-hatred. If history is any guide, it may be enough to attack "radical-liberalism" as a "Jewish conspiracy" in order to put it down. Some Jews will bend to this fear and join their names to Reaction.

Of all the immigrant groups to come to America in the last one hundred years, the Jews have been the most successful economically. Yet, paradoxically, since wealth does not guarantee human fulfillment, our young are among the college youth who have turned their backs most vehemently on America's materialism and riches. While 54.6 percent of the fathers of 1970's incoming Jewish college freshmen are businessmen, only 15 percent of their sons wish to go into business upon graduation.[3] Young Jews are leaders in dissent; they are alienated and angry. In the greater New York City area, the average age of mental patients is twenty-one; of these, 80 percent are middle-class youngsters; 40 percent of the patients are Jews.

Yet, all this is overshadowed by what seems to be a more pressing concern—the fate of the Jews in the Soviet Union and the precarious position of Israel in the Middle East. Survival takes precedence over substantive, radical, spiritual innovation. But the revolution goes on. It will soon demand our primary attention. In this essay, the outlines of that spiritual revolution are sketched.

Jews Are Where the American Middle Class Is Heading

How does one even begin to talk about the Jews and their problems? It appears that we are right now where the upper middle class of America is heading.

Jews earn more per capita than any other ethnic or religious group in America, with the possible exception of Episcopalians, and we shall probably soon pass them. There are not many Jews among America's two hundred

richest families; and there are still many who are desperately poor within our ranks. It is estimated that 6 to
10 percent of Jews in large cities live at the poverty level.
But, generally speaking, Jews have it made.

If education is the key to economic and social eleva-
tion, we are on our way "higher." In this next year, nearly
85 percent of college-age Jews will be matriculated in
universities, as against 42 percent of other white Americans and 23 percent of Blacks.[4] Three times as many
Jews as other Americans will complete college; four times
as many will obtain graduate degrees. At this moment,
three times as many young Jews attending college come
from urban and suburban homes and twice as many receive economic assistance from their parents. We have
fewer children than any other religious or ethnic group.
Indeed, we are "privileged." This is where America aspires
to go, problems and all.

Being part of the upper middle class and well-educated
brings with it great stresses. As many sociologists have
observed, it is the brightest young people who are most
disillusioned by the gap between American ideals and reality, who suspect institutionalized authority, who most
vehemently oppose the Vietnam War. The studies by the
American Council on Education and the United States Office of Education, among others, affirm these findings.[5]

Whereas 27 percent of Protestant and 30 percent of
Catholic college youth favor immediate withdrawal from
Vietnam, this policy is affirmed by 51 percent of Jewish
college students. One-third to one-half of the leaders of
radical protest in Eastern colleges were Jews. Whereas
37 percent of Protestants occasionally or frequently smoke
pot and 43 percent of Catholics, more than two-thirds of
Jewish college youth "turn on" and 24 percent admit to
frequent use of marijuana. One-third of the hippies in
New York's East Village are Jews. Whereas 72 percent of
males and 38 percent of college females who do not smoke

marijuana engage occasionally or frequently in premarital intercourse, 94 percent of the male Jewish "turn-on" students and 86 percent of the females "make it."

The American Council on Education reports that in 1969 27 percent of incoming American college freshmen participated in student demonstrations; but in 1970 41 percent of the incoming freshmen were numbered among the activists. Twice as many incoming college Jewish freshmen protested high school racial policies as did the students of other religions and four times as many Jews protested U. S. military policies.

Pot, sex, radical politics—these are ways some young people say in anger, "Screw you," to an unresponsive society; they are also ways, paradoxically, by which these young people affirm the "juices" of life in an atmosphere that breathes pollution and death.

These statistics in themselves need not cause alarm but they do demand a constructive response. They demonstrate clearly enough that "the times they are a-changin'," as Bob Dylan's folk-rock song puts it.

The New Sexual Morality

While many young Jews are sexually freer than those of former generations, they are not promiscuous. Rescued by this new age from repressive frigidities and overburdened guilt, they are seeking love relationships more authentic than those experienced by their parents. At least they want to talk to those with whom they make love; they want to give and receive the gifts of feelings and self. The small percentage who are promiscuous soon realize that sexuality unrelated to the fulfillment of both body and soul is depersonalizing. They are unhappy persons.

The traditional religious laws of the Jews are the products of a pretechnological, repressive, pre-Freudian, and male dominated era. Although sophisticated in their demand for unity of body and soul, their concern for healthy sexual expression within marriage, their compassion for the unmarried and the compulsive sinner, their acceptance in defined circumstances of birth control, abortion, and divorce—Jewish laws, nevertheless, still are in need of rigorous revision. Some Jews no longer consider masturbation an act of "murder," or would prohibit male participation in birth control, or limit abortion only to cases where the mother's life is threatened, or suggest that homosexuality is a mortal crime. We should no longer accept a double standard in defining adultery or in providing religious relief in divorce cases, nor should we any longer distinguish disparagingly between Jews and non-Jews in sexual responsibility. And, particularly, since we no longer encourage early marriage, we must, in this age of "the pill," reconsider our teachings on premarital chastity.

I propose that a major effort be made to rewrite guidelines that would set forth Jewish ideals as they relate to contemporary sexual behavior. These guidelines must be products of research and consultation that will include not only rabbinical experts in Talmudic law, but psychologists, sociologists, lawyers, doctors, parents, and youth. These sexual codes should not be based merely on the exegesis of selected biblical phrases but rather on a realistic understanding of the phases of human growth and fulfillment.

The Drug Culture and Marijuana

Many young Jews have experimented with pot; a small percentage have become addicted to hard drugs. The heroin problem is an urgent one and requires an intelligent response. This should include medical, social, and psychological treatment for the user and severe punishment for pushers.

Any sophisticated analysis of the drug culture, however, must distinguish between "horse," "acid," and "pot."

The Jewish Community

To treat their use as equally sinful is to compound the mistrust of young people.

Jews are abandoning the mind-expanding drugs, mescaline, LSD, etc., now that their danger has been clearly demonstrated. But marijuana appears to be here to stay. Despite the stereotype, most Jewish college students I know who "turn on" with grass are also deeply involved in political action or have adopted counterculture life-styles. Marijuana is even less a "cop out" for them than dry martinis are for adults. In 1969 Americans consumed more than three billion sleeping pills and downed two hundred million dollars worth of tranquilizers. But that is no excuse. We must ask ourselves why it is that in order to live in this society both adults and youngsters in such large numbers seem to need artificial help.

We must also face up to the question as to whether repression of marijuana is not, after all, a treacherous attack on those whose life-style is an implicit condemnation of the establishment's status quo—values and politics. The long-haired college student has become today's "nigger," and marijuana laws have been used as a contrived means of oppressing him.

Laws restricting the use of marijuana should be reconsidered. That done, I shall urge my fellow Jews to achieve their "highs" through authentic encounters with life and within interpersonal relations. But this requires also that we lessen the competitiveness of our society, provide greater psychic security for our young, and strengthen the support that comes from meaningful participation in authentic community. Repressive laws will not resolve this crisis, but the reconstruction of our value system will help.

I recall the insights of Allen Y. Cohen, a former pupil and follower of Dr. Timothy Leary, and presently Professor of Psychology and Dean of Men at the experimental John F. Kennedy University near Berkeley, California. For four years a "psychedelic utopian" who "dropped" LSD more than thirty times (it did him no permanent harm), Dr. Cohen confesses, "No matter how good the experiences were, we always came down and nothing really changed inside." Drug experiences, he notes, are "dreamlike" and obstacles to "real awareness." "There are ways to discover the fountain of inner happiness. But the use of drugs is not one of them." Dr. Cohen urges that hard drug pushers be "busted," drug users provided with "rehabilitation, prevention and sympathy." He concludes: "Drugs are not the problem. Life is the problem. People are the problem. . . . The challenge of the age is to provide young people with alternative possibilities to develop themselves on the physical, sensory, emotional, intra-personal, creative, aesthetic, intellectual, social and political and spiritual levels by nonchemical means."[6] Regretfully, Jewish religious institutions have hardly begun to work at such an important program.

Dissent and Violence

Many young Jews are cynical about America's democratic processes, particularly as it concerns the Vietnam War, black justice, and student participation in academic planning. But they distinguish properly between constructive dissent and violent revolution. Only a few Jews are among the S.D.S.-Weatherman-type bombers. Jews have too long a heritage of nonviolence and too great a respect for persons to withstand the guilt of the murder of innocents and the futile destruction of property. Only a very shortsighted or sick student will fail to anticipate the counterrepression that revolutionary violence produces. The radical Jews—even though their despair is deep—do not consider such violence productive, and rightly suspect that those who use destructive means are really destroying their own humanity, sensitivity, and compassion.

Nevertheless, we must understand that the violence of an unresponsive, racist, war-oriented society inevitably produces such a tragic violence of its own. The children of violence are the products of our own murderous misuse of technology.

Those radicals who are committed to Judaism are involved in organizing communes, fellowships, and free universities. In order to open American and Jewish institutions to a reassessment of priorities and programs, they are planning dialogue, encounter, demonstration and, if necessary, dissenting disruption. Admittedly, they are antagonistic to the Jewish community, as it is now structured, but they are hungering for Jewish experiences—and they are experimenting on their own.[7] Only too gradually Jewish adults are hearing these young radicals and tentatively, begrudgingly, and fearfully our institutions are responding.

I urge strongly that young people be invited at every level of institutional decision-making to participate, not as token representatives, but as full and responsible members. We need their voices in order to call us back to sanity, in order to help us plan for tomorrow's world.

Changes are required in theology and liturgy, structural organization, education, and the substance of our programming. Some innovations are evident in all these areas.

Changes in Jewish Theology and Synagogue Practice

Mordecai Kaplan's theological definitions have become part of the "folk religion" of American Jews, as Charles Liebman verifies in his 1970 American Jewish Committee, Jewish Publication Society Year Book study of American rabbis, synagogues, and organizational presidents. Jews now realize that religion is not to be defined by laws allegedly revealed by a supernaturalist God or written in a book, or as articulated by an ecclesiastical committee of rabbi-scholars. Religion is rather the process by which an entire people find meaning in their historic experiences or attribute meaning to that experience; and then through rites and ceremonies, corporate liturgy, they struggle with, celebrate, and communicate the values implicit in their encounter with reality. Religion is always open to new experience, it is dynamic and transforming, it mediates past verities and tomorrow's dreams.

Today's God is not the biblical "Who," the Lord Yahweh, who dried up the sea of reeds, who exiled and rescued, who fashioned miracles, who brought low and raised up. Nor is God the rabbinic "What" of Greek-influenced philosophy whose elements and attributes once provoked the attention of rational concern.

God is immanent and in process. It is *godness* which is within those experiences of persons and nations in history that presses us always to experience our humanity as authentic. It is *godness* which drives us to create social conditions of justice and peace. This "God as process" is "transcendent" in the sense that man's need to find meaning in life and to live it with dignity is part of the divine-givenness of our creatureliness. It was experienced by Adam, and we know it now as the concern of our young. In each generation we are obliged to reassess both the values we share and the symbols by which we communicate those values. As the Midrash wisely taught, each generation of men must affirm God anew and each man can know God only according to his strength.

Inevitably some synagogues, mostly empty except for "year-end" Jews, are exploring new forms of worship. In prayer we ought to say what we believe. We ought to say it in ways that stimulate our minds and inspire our hearts. Multi-million-dollar sanctuaries, plush seats, passive congregations, sterile prayer books—these are giving way to small, simple structures, dialogue sermons, guitars as well as organs, readings selected from the best of contemporary literature, dramatic skits and dances, loose-leaf prayer books. Not all of the new liturgy is effective or successful, but liturgy-building, after all, is a lifelong procedure. Its value lies more in what we are trying to do and who is doing it than in what we actually achieve. But, there is at last a stirring in this direction.

One problem with "God as process" theology is the need to distinguish between that in man which is humane and that human perversity which uses even the best in us to seduce, manipulate, and dominate. Man is capable of cruelty in unusual ways. Control over technology now gives man the capacity for evil in an ultimate apocalyptic dimension. Thus, our counterculture groups insist on nonstandardization, on smallness, on the weakness of centralized authority. They want to touch that part of the self that responds mystically both to the enduring past in history and to the hope of future human self-realization. They also want to overcome the depersonalization and alienation fostered by our society and achieve instead a new form of free personhood and meaningful community. We have seen in some synagogues, therefore, a paradoxical combination of the old traditions and new styles of communication: large prayer shawls along with strobe lights, Hasidic chants along with incense and guitars at parlor services where students sit huddled on the floor and share their prayer books, or at lakeside retreats, at outdoor gatherings or as part of social-action demonstrations. It is in this area of liturgical development that our young people have been most innovative and most successful.

In the Reconstructionist Movement, many of our synagogues—there are fifteen synagogues and twelve fellowships—use the prayer book sparingly. Dialogue, education, discussion, dramatic readings, the recitation of more relevant literature—these are intermingled with the ancient rites. We also have a number of fellowships, small groups of families, some of whom belong to synagogues and some of whom would never find themselves in "sanctuary." Parents and children together conduct services that reflect on the values that emerge out of their weekly parlor-centered education and discussion.

I encourage such "underground" study groups; I also urge the division of large synagogue membership into functional cell groups, all of whom would seek through liturgy to communicate the holiest of their experiences.

The division of synagogue groups into men's clubs and women's groups, the young marrieds, college and high school youth—these are all the product of Reform Judaism's imitation of American Protestantism. In Europe, our societies instead conformed to those functions that grew out of pressing and realistic need: a society to visit the sick, raise dowries for the bride, rescue captives, negotiate with the government, recite prayers for the dead, study Torah. I propose that once again we restructure the synagogue into such small functional groups that will include adults and young—one for study, another to work for Israel, a third for work in the ghetto, a fourth to provide draft counseling, and so on. Each group might then assume responsibility for the development of a liturgy that will communicate the values inherent in the commune's experience with life itself. As of old, services might be freely interrupted in order to provide a hearing for dissent. Through question and answer and by dialogue, the Torah reading might again become a lesson in the application of the scriptural word to life's ongoing challenge, instead of a boring singsong of past events. There is much in the Torah that still edifies us. Most importantly, also, its study helps us to know who we were and how we developed. It provides us with roots in the past and enables us to grow, secure in our identity as a Jewish people. Prayer, newly composed, might articulate values germinating from the gut experience of our people's confrontation with life. By that process, we give meaning to life or at least try to make sense out of it.

But I question whether we ought to place all our hope in the weekly prayer service at a given edifice, no matter how well reconstructed. Certainly there is value in a service which links us to the past, contains elements that are repeated week after week, and includes ceremonies in Hebrew, a language of universal Jewish applicability. Thus, a Jew—in moments of stress or joy—might enter a synagogue anywhere in the world and participate in a known ceremony that would join his spiritual life to that of our ancestors, our Jewish community, and our hopes for mankind. This is a form of holiness that we should not so simply cast aside. But, on the other hand, if liturgy is to be functionally related to the "now" problems of today's life, we need to create occasions not necessarily in any one designated edifice but anywhere, not once a week but at appropriate moments—for a week at a time, or for a whole month, for an intensive weekend, or whatever. During such a period, we would join prayer to study, to research in the community, to social action, to conflict, debate, and encounter, to innovative experiments in opening ourselves to human sensitivity, using a fluid art form that should include verbal and nonverbal forms of communication and ceremony. Both "these and these" are ways to experience God.

Changing the Methods of Religious Education

The Sunday school of Reform Judaism, even as the Talmud Torah methods of Orthodox Judaism, are failures. Jewish education reaches more Jewish youth today than ever before, but it is infantile, elementary, painfully boring. It turns countless Jewish young off. Less than 10 percent continue beyond the age of thirteen. It is a miracle that so many young Jews still wish to maintain their allegiance, despite the torture they endured called "Hebrew school." Fortunately there are new methods to which our young are responding: language laboratories and elementary school play groups; Hebrew arts groups, summer camps, and retreats where the whole environment supports the educational process; travel to Israel and work on the soil where prophets once trod and our people struggle still to live and create democracy; academically sound course offerings in the university, radical social action communes and their publications. These are the new directions for Jewish education.

Jews still spend about one hundred twenty dollars per child for elementary religious school "torture" and only about fifteen dollars for college-age youth. We import almost half our advanced Hebrew teachers from abroad. Yet our Jewish federations still hold back the funding required by higher Jewish education, camping, Israel-sponsored trips, teacher training institutions, and Jewish scholarship. Jewish youth have responded to this obscene denial with their own youth-directed "free universities," with counterculture college youth groups, and with havurot or fellowships alongside the major seminaries. At last Hillel, the Jewish centers, and Jewish federations are experimenting with staff who are not edifice-centered but reach out instead to the young and minister to them wherever they will be: in dormitories, at demonstrations, in the Haight-Ashburys and East Villages.

Most pointedly, Jewish youth have little patience with the denominational structures that sought loyalty to sectarian institutions even before providing comprehension of the universal values to which we should be dedicated. More and more Jewish education must overcome the suffocating grip of denominational establishments and return to community schools and Jewish ecumenical experience.

I propose a moratorium on elementary Jewish education and suggest instead a year-long reassessment by rabbis, educators, parents, and children on which forms of education should receive our major support, what we ought to teach, and how to go about it. I would particularly like to give our children a chance to tell the parents "where it's at." We have the intelligence to do better and it is time we used that intelligence.

Changing the Program of Jewish Organizations

Jewish organizations outside of synagogue control were created to serve sectarian and frequently defensive Jewish needs: Jewish hospitals to provide for kosher-observant Jews and doctors denied internship elsewhere; Jewish centers for the Americanization of our immigrants and social recreation; the Anti-Defamation League, the American Jewish Committee, the American Jewish Congress, to fight anti-Semitism; Jewish federations to coordinate fund-raising; Zionist organizations to win the Jewish state and secure its existence.

These needs are still well-represented and powerfully entrenched. Many of them are still functionally significant. There is no democratically organized Jewish forum, however, where a radical reassessment of needs can take place and priorities be rearranged. Thus, work for peace, involvement in the black thrust for justice, an adjustment of traditional Jewish teachings on sexuality, support for counterculture youth groups—these receive low priority in Jewish communal concern. Besides, it is difficult to argue with the heavy hand of status and old traditions. The moneys of the Jewish community are apportioned roughly according to the favorite interests of those German Jews who came to America first. It is almost impossible for new causes to be financed unless they are absorbed, modified, and then controlled by the established power structure. Furthermore, the evocation of an anti-Semitic threat or the genuinely pressing needs of Israel for guns, speak more compellingly than a campaign to achieve selective conscientious objection or the provocative proposal to do away with "merit tests" and replace some Jews long waiting for administrative posts in public schools with blacks, Puerto Ricans, and Chicanos.

On the central issue of the Vietnam War, many Jews honestly believe that the battle against communist influence in the Middle East is linked inextricably with the battle against communist infiltration in the Far East. They are incapable, regrettably, of distinguishing between various forms of communism; nor do they recognize the military establishment's motivations in this simple equation, so eager are they for American support for Israel. One does not easily criticize an administration from whom one wishes favors.

Left-inspired attacks on Israel's policies toward Palestinian extremists who appear hell-bent on a murder course regrettably have cut off dialogue. The Jewish establishment and radical Jewish critics of Israel's political policies are at this moment shouting past each other, at least in America. There is much greater freedom for political dissent in Israel and a wider range of options are there publicly articulated. The Jewish Peace Fellowship—a long-established pacifist organization in America—has been forced to fire its staff for lack of funds. Jewish Defense Agencies sought to silence a respected Israeli critic who offered alternative proposals for Israel's political dilemmas.

There are some changes on the horizon. Jewish community centers and Jewish federations at this late date have begun to examine the racism and the obstacles within the Jewish community that prevent a more aggressive, institutionalized Jewish involvement in the Black Power thrust. The American Jewish Congress and the Anti-Defamation League have set up meager programs in black-Jewish dialogue. Some money is going to rescue Jewish businessmen in black ghettoes and turn over the businesses. Some Jewish organizations are involved in head-start education, job-training, and the counseling of black capitalists. A few rabbis here and there support black community control of schools, businesses, police, and political power—but they are still too few!

Let us tell the truth: Jews fear the violence they know to be in the black community. There is much of white prejudice among Jews. The reluctance of Jews, who have fled the cities and live in the suburbs, to involve themselves more than patronizingly in black political efforts has placed a restraint on Jewish organizational leaders who might be willing to do more. Jews wish Blacks would conduct their campaign "our way," i.e., by repressing their hostility, using the system against itself through hard work and education. So Jews reveal how little aware they are of the violent, destructive, and cruel American attack on the black man's integrity. We know our own history of suffering well, and we console ourselves in it, but we are grossly ignorant of the black man's history. We turn our face from the bloodletting, the castration of the Black, and we justify our prejudice with curdling tales of black injustices directed against us.

The Jewish community must be challenged, therefore, to a drastically more urgent and resourceful involvement in a Black-Jewish alliance that should eventually include the white ethnics and the lower middle classes. We are obliged by all our values to engage in a persistent assault on the complacency and racism of an American society that approves only half-measures to overcome the problems of poverty and urban decay. These problems will assuredly dehumanize us and destroy our civilization if we are not more compassionate and militant. Jews serve their own interests when they ally themselves to the black man's rightful quest for justice.

Reform Jewish leadership and the American Jewish Congress, particularly, have led in the attack on the Vietnam War. They have urged draft counseling and selective conscientious objection laws. But the effect of this political muscle is weakened by dissent in the ranks.

Radical Jewish youth, therefore, have been compelled to do their own thing in race relations and in opposition to the misuse of American military power. They are doing it outside the structures of the Jewish community. Some Jewish organizations are reconsidering their obduracy. B'nai B'rith's Hillel, which long included youth on their board, is now considering the possibility that Hillel might house Jewish campus groups with a wide variety of political positions, including those not now approved by B'nai B'rith. The American Jewish Committee has provided teasingly small sums to enable radical Jewish youth to circulate their own publications. The committee has also engaged staff who will work with Jewish youth in developing the free university movement.

Pluralism, Community, and Polarization

The issue confronting the Jewish community is how to confine the polarization which is inevitable from the sharp differences on these political issues and support properly the pluralism within our ranks. Indeed, this is the problem confronted by all of humanity: how to structure life so that we can dissent, quarrel with each other, and yet affirm our corporate humanity. If a religious community that shares a history, a symbol system, a corporate sense of destiny, cannot find the way, how will the world? This challenge ought to motivate radical and conservative Jewish leaders to a more urgent dialogue with each other; regretfully it has not yet.

I urge that we encourage all points of view within the Jewish community to organize themselves and to propagate their opinions; that community funds and forums be available to all; and that we structure dialogue and debate within our programming at every level of institution. Although we shall be pulled in many directions, I have faith in Truth, if it can be freely articulated. Furthermore, I believe that the vitality we shall experience when youth and adults at the grass roots know that they will be heard, will more than compensate for the anguish of division.

Right now power is in the hands of a selected few bureaucrats, agency professionals, and their handpicked, wealthy supporters. There is little chance to influence Jewish life except through the manipulation of such established organizations and a policy of currying the favor of the powerful administrators. We have no pope but the established Jewish community can silently excommunicate, defame, destroy, and censor opposition as effectively as any authoritarian regime, if not more so. It can also provide fantastic support to any project it favors. Thus I plead with the Jewish establishment, in order to save its own soul and protect our corporate future, that it be willing to encourage, even support, the dissent of the nonestablishment, nonaffiliated, radical alternative. At this moment, the alternative Jewish society, probably, includes the majority of our young. Opening our community structures to their concerns is the most important revolution in which radical Jews committed to Jewish life can engage.

Although I stand with the radical youth, I will not leave the Jewish people as some of them already have. There is no other place to go. Communes in Taos cannot support all the potential drop-outs and, furthermore, man carries his finiteness and his perversity with him everywhere. I am aware that bitter division exists even in the ranks of the "drop-outs." I must shape my world, therefore, where I am—that means for me, within the Jewish community, within America, within Israel, within the world of nations.

The Role of the Academy

At the Reconstructionist Rabbinical College, we are experimenting with a new theology, structure, and substantive program. Our students are engaged in ecumenical studies in a state-supported university, we live in the ghetto, we allow for a wide variety of liturgical expression and personal life-styles, we urge social action as an extension of religious study.[8]

Once when the Jewish people were confronted with the tragic destruction of their temple in Jerusalem and the political authority of their commonwealth, when chaos, anarchy, and disorder were rampant, they were rescued at last by a rabbinical academy at Yabne. When violence had reached the point of ruin, the return of a few scholars to community, contemplation, study, and prayer, the heroism of these daring pioneers, was enough.

In Boston, New York, Philadelphia, Washington, Chicago, Los Angeles, Berkeley—in Jerusalem, too—young Jews and their rabbis, informed adults and innocent newcomers to the ranks, have committed themselves to a new style of Jewish living, study, prayer, and social involvement. There have been established havurot, new seminaries, free universities, radical Jewish social-action groups. There is much hope to be gained from the existence of such groups.

We are in exile everywhere—even in Israel—and we seek our "home." We shall find it in the God pulsating within and through compassion for the tears of others. We shall become ourselves when we know that to be Jewish is to be truly human and that there can be no salvation for ourselves unless the world itself is redeemed. Particularly in the Jewish state, there will be no security until justice is achieved for all, both the Jew and the Palestinian; and all must renounce violence as the means of social change.

Zion and the State of Israel

My revered teacher, Mordecai Kaplan, placed "Zion" at the center of his concern, not the State of Israel. Zion symbolizes all the dreams and hopes of the Jew for a world at peace. For the Jew, the State of Israel is a necessary component in the making of such a world. The State is not identical to Zion but is rather our effort to give the ideal form. We shall not let Christian hostility to our particularism or earth-rootedness deter us. Indeed, we hope for Christian understanding. Although my concerns are universal, I believe that the Jewish people have the right, in fact, are *required,* to demonstrate how our religious convictions shape the structures of society. Religion has no meaning if it does not confront, specifically, problems of power, social justice, majority-minority relations, economic distribution, church-state alliance, war and peace. It is through "ethical nationhood" that the world will find its way to international community.

The State of Israel must be secular, in the sense that no church is favored and all men are equal before the law. Even though it will be secular, the State will still have meaning for me because there Jews—as the majority of the population—will influence the culture and determine the prevailing mores and value system. For that reason, I oppose leftist proposals for a binational state where Jewish cultural influences will be submerged in a pan-Arab world. Israel must be in the Arab world, but it must maintain the integrity of its own particular vision.

I do not believe in missionary campaigns. I believe that a people influences the world not by distributing tracts but by the example of their lives. That is why Israel is so important to me. There Jews will be tested on "the rack" of history. There we have an opportunity to be a "light to the nations." I believe that "salvation" is achieved not only by individual worthiness and by faith but also by the kind of society individuals make together. Only in Israel do Jews have the power to determine, as Jews, the *Jewish* quality of the society. In America, Jews are gadflies, and our task is essentially defensive. We are irritants.

In Israel, Jews can be more genuinely creative. Yet both are necessary since Israel is politically impotent and America is overwhelming.

Trapped between its own doves and hawks, squeezed between Russia and America, the resolution of Israel's problems requires of the State's leaders an awareness of the tension between the ideal Zion and the Jewish State. World peace and the security of the State are functions of each other. Military might spares for a moment. It may not be abandoned. Justice makes peace. Hopefully, alternative solutions will be found by the Israelis, Palestinians, Arabs, Russians, and Americans.

Caught between a past tradition that is revered as word of God, and a radical youthful lunge—often careless and unthinking—into the future, squeezed between a defensive concern for Jewish safety and the desperate call for radical action to save all mankind, the American Jew must also find his way.

The truth is out: each man must find his salvation in his own place; and there is no salvation for any man until the world itself is redeemed.

Future Prospects

If my analysis of the present situation of the Jewish community is accurate, then we are in for hard times. We may experience the apocalypse in our own time. But I do not really believe that America needs to be rescued by violent revolution, nor do I believe that Israel will find her ultimate security in jet planes, nor that the Jewish community will be strengthened merely by condemnatory denunciation. The prophetic literature endured, but the prophets—according to our folk-legends—all suffered violent deaths; their messages rarely converted the leaders for long. I trust, therefore, that I am proposing a more effective, more radical approach to life-making.

The Jewish Community

The course of violence must end with death. If change is to come, I hope it will come because Jews who care, by their life-styles and through the institutions they themselves create, will offer a viable alternative. The future can be determined by the peaceful, radical revolution already in process. It might be delayed, but I do not believe it will be defeated. It is the future for which I hope.

NOTES

1. Mordecai M. Kaplan, *Judaism as a Civilization* (New York: Schocken, 1967; first published 1934), and idem, *The Meaning of God in Modern Jewish Religion* (New York: Reconstructionist Press, 1967; first published 1937).

2. See these most recent books on this theme: Eugene Borowitz, *Choosing a Sex Ethic* (New York: Schocken Books, 1969); David M. Feldman, *Birth Control in Jewish Law* (New York: New York University Press, 1968) ; Richard L. Rubenstein, *Morality and Eros* (New York: McGraw Hill, 1970).

3. The statistics in this essay are drawn from the following studies: David E. Drew, *A Profile of the Jewish Freshman,* American Council on Education Research Report (Washington, D.C.) Vol. 5, No. 4, 1970; *Playboy Magazine,* September 1970; *What We Know about Young American Jews* (New York: American Jewish Committee, 1970).

4. *New York Times,* October 10, 1970, and reports by B'nai B'rith Hillel Foundation, Washington, D.C.

5. Some significant studies on student dissent include the following by the American Council on Education:
"Campus Tensions: Analysis and Recommendations," Report on the Special Committee on Campus Tensions, Research Report, April 1970; "Social Issues and Protest Activities: Recent Student Trends," A.C.E. Research Report, February 1970; "Campus Disruption 1968-1969: An Analysis of the Causal Factors, Psychology and Problems of Society," *Educational Record,* Fall 1969; "Black and White Freshmen Entering Four Year Colleges," *Educational Record,* Fall 1969.
Additional significant studies on student dissent, are:
"The Scranton Report on Campus Unrest" in *Chronicle of Higher Education,* Washington, D.C., October 5, 1970; United

What the Religious Revolutionaries Are Saying

States Office of Education Report on High School Unrest, prepared by the Policy Institute of Syracuse University, October 1970, reported in *New York Times,* October 4, 1970; Report of the American Bar Association Commission on Campus Government and Campus Dissent (Chicago, 1970) ; Carnegie Commission on Higher Education, Report on Campus Disorders following Cambodian Invasion, October 1970, reported in *New York Times,* October 3, 1970; Report of commission preparing for 1971 White House Conference on Youth, reported in *New York Post,* September 15, 1970; House Sub-Committee on General Education, Report on Student Protests at Public and Private High Schools, February 1970; President's Commission on Campus Unrest, Survey on Student Disorders prepared by Urban Institute, Washington, D.C., reported in *New York Times,* November 4, 1970; Center for Research and Education in American Liberties at Teachers College Columbia University, Report on high school students' attitudes in New York and Philadelphia for United States Office of Education, September 1970.

6. *Religious News Service,* October 13, 1970.

7. A description of Jewishly-committed radical youth groups will be found in articles that have appeared regularly in *Response,* a contemporary Jewish review, 415 South Street, Waltham, Mass. 02154.

8. For additional information on the Reconstructionist Rabbinical College, write to 15 W. 86th Street, New York, N. Y. 10024, or 2304 N. Broad St., Philadelphia, Pa. 19132.

ABOUT
THE UNIVERSITY

EDWARD L. LEE, JR.

The student stormed out of the dean's office, his face and manner revealing anger and frustration. As he passed a campus minister friend in the hall, he blurted out bluntly, "This damn place is just like the church. It never practices what it preaches!" And without waiting for reaction or reply he continued down the hall, flung open the door, and exclaimed, "Who needs it?"

Adolescent impatience? Perhaps. Dated clichés? Probably. Overworked student rhetoric? Probably not—because nothing in the worst of current inflammatory jargon quite matches for meaninglessness the rhetoric employed by institutions of higher learning to describe their purposes or justify their goals. Rhetoric, once a revered and respected academic discipline, is now through its misuse both a clue and an index to the problems which plague the college and university.

The art of rhetoric was once required of students because it was regarded as an essential skill by which the individual articulated and communicated ideas and feelings with other persons. It was assumed that the language and skill of rhetoric were commensurate with the subjects and problems and values it was talking about. It was granted that this verbal vehicle was not only in touch with the realities it sought to describe, but that those realities in turn could be known and experienced by the sheer excellence of rhetoric. Talk was not cheap in the university. But today it is, and rhetoric has become a pejorative word; it means the contrived language of public relations, no longer the language of learning.

Church persons know a familiar parallel to this situation. Preaching is the church's rhetoric and it suffers the same affliction which plagues rhetoric in the university. Once preaching was the honored discipline of homiletics, the verbal art of proclaiming the gospel, "truth through personality" as Phillips Brooks defined and practiced it. And at its best preaching was regarded as a gospel event, the verbal dialogue between proclaimer and gospel which was not simply a description of divine reality but a disclosure and experience of it. Who approaches preaching in that manner and with that expectation today? It, too, is now a pejorative word, a discipline misused because it is frequently out of touch with the realities of God and man and the world it is supposed to know and convey.

Rhetoric and homiletics: quaint words and irrelevant practices of academe and ecclesia which are judged out of touch and out of favor. One is accused of not practicing what it preaches, the other with not practicing what it teaches. In a word, hypocrisy—and it makes no difference whether it is intentional or unintentional. It is now regarded as inevitable. No matter what bright, imaginative, and creative person assumes the post of dean or president in a college or university, it is cynically asserted that before long he or she will start talking and posturing in a way determined by the job and not primarily by the individual's ideas about the job. It can be argued that in the university it is inevitable that the idealistic and unrealistic expectations of most students and some faculty, when juxtaposed to the daily functional necessities of the institution, will always evoke some kind of irreconcilable tension and potential conflict. But the problem today is more serious than that. The charge of inevitable hypocrisy is challenging the university's self-understanding and its traditional method of operation.

It is still commonly assumed that the purpose and task of the university is to clear space and create a setting conducive to the independent exercise of the human mind by qualified intellectuals. In that autonomous context they are to pursue that elusive entity known as "truth" which, when converted into manageable and marketable knowledge, shall be dispensed to society as a whole for its benefit and welfare. But notice what else is assumed, namely, that what goes on in that space and setting is a privilege for those whom the university deems qualified and chooses to admit and eventually either reject or reward. The university, according to this academic model, is a caretaker and a custodian of truth and knowledge, the possessor of that special mystique known as "learning." It is a model which assumes and promotes intellectual elitism. It prevailed in most colleges and universities in pre-World War II America and is still the main working model in higher education today. The problem is that this elitist model is increasingly out of touch with the needs of the nation and the world today.

Post-World War II America is an essentially urban, technological society, indelibly afflicted with systemic pollution, poverty, and racism. It has also unleashed nuclear energy, taken the initial steps of exploring space, and introduced an unprecedented era of instant global communication by means of electronic media which have successfully competed with verbalization as the means of human communication. Higher education, operating on the elitist model, has been very instrumental in all of this. But it now seems clear that education and learning *in* and *for* this kind of society can no longer be elitist: that is, a privilege for the properly qualified. It has to become egalitarian, a right for everyone, based upon a new understanding of what it means to be qualified.

To an extent higher education in America has already recognized this. The rapid development of state systems of higher education such as those in New York and California, the overnight emergence of numerous tax-supported two-year community colleges, the deliberate attempt to create experimental colleges committed to testing new models of education, and the extensive expansion in space and enrollments by urban commuter universities have had the result that commuting to school is fast replacing the residential college as the norm in American higher education.

But the issue is more basic than mere size and numbers. If the American university is going to shift from an elitist model of education to an egalitarian model, then it must understand that its function is no longer that of caretaker and custodian of truth and knowledge, a tight little island of wisdom in the midst of larger oceans of ignorance. Rather, the egalitarian model requires the implementation of a new set of assumptions as to what constitutes teaching and learning, governing and decision-making, power and social usefulness.

It is precisely at this point that the transition is failing. The university as an institution continues to use the rhetoric and criteria of the elitist model to publicize and program itself with the consequence that it has little relation to what is or ought to be going on. What has developed is a frustrating dichotomy between the university as an actual place of learning and the university as an institution which attempts to manage and manipulate the processes of learning along traditional elitist lines. An examination of some of the university's rhetoric will reveal this.

Learning is the primary business of the university. In the abstract, few would argue with this. But when the questions of learning for whom and for what are raised, the argument begins. The university continues to rely upon the least effective means of learning motivation and achievement: reward and punishment in combination with competition and passivity. The student is treated as a separate entity who must be talked at, tested, examined, graded, and scaled by previously qualified superiors. Learning is intake rather than interaction, a one-way action by the custodian of truth which assumes a blotter model according to which the student can absorb and obtain knowledge handed down by a more knowledgable person. It is forced feeding rather than natural digestion. Regurgitation might please teachers and gain high marks, but more often than not it results in little nourishment. One student has aptly expressed it:

> I had a growing sense that these numbers and letters—which supposedly measured something in a supposedly precise way —had little or nothing to do with my mind's activity or learning. They seemed quite capricious and arbitrary in relation to anything I experienced. It might be the case that high school grades and S.A.T. scores could indicate college grades which in turn predicted Graduate Record scores, etc. But I could not imagine what this strange symbolic rigamarole had to do with anything outside itself: when all the rich and varied information about ability, performance, interest, etc., that went into the academic system emerged as a pseudo-precise ranking scheme.

Testing, grading, and ranking might have been a legitimate prod for learning in the elitist era of education when knowledge was dispensed to the unknowing and it was agreed that the university had a prior grasp of reliable information and reasonable truth. But that is no longer necessarily true. Any undergraduate who has traveled or read independently, or simply watched the cosmic eye of television, brings to the classroom a data bank of raw information, first-hand experiences, and intuitive feelings which have already instigated a good deal of learning in the student. All this is too often dismissed or ignored by professors as unreliable and unreasonable. It does not fit predetermined categories or theories. Furthermore, it is difficult to grade. The student is regarded as essentially uninformed; the teacher would rather start from his own beginning instead of the point where his expertise and the student's inquisitive awareness can interest and inform each other. But this latter is what the egalitarian model of higher education requires.

The traditional authoritarian relationship whereby teacher controls student is no longer viable. Either teaching and learning is a mutual process of investigation, discovery, sharing, and respect, unencumbered by artificial requirements and rewards, or it is not really teaching and learning at all. If nothing else, this must be the common point of departure in the university classroom. It will not guarantee learning but in all likelihood it will give it a better chance than is its current possibility.

The university is an academic community. This usually indicates a community of scholars engaged in a mutual and interdependent pursuit of knowledge and truth. Already this has a hollow ring to it. It is probably more accurate to describe it as a conglomerate of interrelated power blocks each looking out for its own self-interest. The group with the least power is the student body; yet this is the basic constituency of the university. Traditional elitist rhetoric affirms that the university exists primarily for the student, but today one wonders whether in the long run the student is not essentially a pawn in the power games of others.

Strictly speaking, a community of scholars is basically the faculty, whose professional stakes in the university are immense and deeply felt. The tenured faculty have made it for keeps and their personal power and prestige is considered their just reward for having successfully mastered and survived the academic credentials race. At its best this academic autonomy for the faculty is an important mandate: to pursue and challenge and advocate all ideas with vigor and excellence, free from the hostile whims and pressures of those who might be offended. But too often this mandate has degenerated into a business-as-usual mentality characterized by a preoccupation with personal and departmental empires while allowing others in the university to make the decisions about the character and nature of education.

As long as these professional empires are not threatened the faculty are more than likely to remain uninvolved in the larger life of the university, even though historically the shaping of the university has been jealously regarded as one of their chief prerogatives. When the Cox Commission evaluated the role of the faculty at Columbia University in the aftermath of the 1968 student uprisings, it said: ". . . The faculty became more and more remote from the problems of student life and general university policy not related to formal instruction. The authoritarian manner, on one side, and aloofness, on the other, were mutually reinforcing."[1] In varying degrees this describes most university faculties in this country.

The other components in the power structure of the so-called academic community are the administrators and trustees; one must also take account of the power of state legislators. The rapid growth and expansion of higher education in America, if nothing else, means it is big business with political connections and consequences. This new arrangement has thoroughly secularized the old academy but it has also played havoc with decision-making in the ivory tower. Enough evidence already exists to show that trustees are in general "a group of middle-aged Republican businessmen of a moderate-conservative cast, reluctant to accent principles of academic freedom, opposed to giving students and faculty members a major role in campus decisions, and poorly read in the field of higher education."[2] Nevertheless, here is the locus of real power in the university today. To exercise it and at the same time juggle the daily tasks and demands of running the university is that beleaguered group known as administrators.

What the Religious Revolutionaries Are Saying

Administrators are ambivalent academics: their sympathies incline them toward the classroom and learning, but their jobs are to run a successful corporation and call it an academic community. They know where the real power is and quite often they wish it were elsewhere. The basic constituency, the student body, is disfranchised; the group which claims to have the legitimate power, the faculty, rarely exercises it; the trustees do not hesitate to wield power that they assume is rightly theirs. As a consequence, administrators are not above playing one group against another in order to preserve their own power in the university.

The issue, of course, is who should govern the university. The elitist model of education maintains that the university is governed from above, endowers-alumni-legislators-prestigious folk from the outside and tenured faculty from within. In the earlier elitist era of truly private universities and colleges this autocratic hierarchy could with some reason justify its legitimacy to govern higher education. Today that justification is gone. The egalitarian needs of higher education and society require the university to commit itself to students as its primary and most important constituency and to give substance to that commitment to incorporate them at every level of governance, in most instances with equal power and in some with majority power. An honest and legitimate community, academic and otherwise, is not one which orders itself on the basis of good will and intentions while vested interests call the shots. Rather, it is one which distributes power fairly to those who are indispensable to its purposes and functioning. In the university this means first and foremost the student. The student should have voice and vote in all matters which bear most directly upon his education: academic requirements, course content, curriculum structures, departmental structures, faculty evaluation, administrative appointments, discipline codes. What is the student's responsibility after

granting him this governance right and power? It is no
different than for anyone else who exercises power: to do
it justly and intelligently. When students can count for
something in the university, it might turn out that a more
genuine academic community will emerge.

The university as an institution in society is neutral. This
is a deceptive piece of rhetoric. It states that in order for
the university to provide total and unfettered academic
freedom for its individual members it must as an institution maintain a neutral position on issues and crises facing
society at large. In short, it cannot take sides officially.

In principle this seems logical. In practice, however, it
does not quite work out that way. The maintenance of neutrality by the university has resulted in the development
and cultivation of highly valuable neutral academic skills:
value-free detachment, objective analysis, dispassionate investigation, bias-free research, functional and pragmatic
technological expertise. Technotronic America has an in-
satiable need and market for these particular skills. To the
extent that they are in great demand by agriculture, all levels
of government, the space industries, the military, banking
and business, the health sciences, labor and industry, the
university gathers to itself unique and special power in
society. The dependence of public institutions on higher
education with its research centers, skills development, and
information capability means that the university has the
opportunity to exercise deliberate and significant influence
on the purposes and values of these institutions. But what
happens is that on a basis of professed neutrality the
university confers its power and prestige uncritically, with
the result that it finds itself hyphenated to some very un-
neutral enterprises; the military-industrial-academic complex, for instance. In other words, this so-called neutral
power of the university gets co-opted by others whose interests and purposes are by no means neutral. It all smacks
of conspiracy, but more often than not it begins as a con-

tract of convenience: the neutral research skills of the university sought and paid for by enterprises which are utterly dependent on the data and skills which the university can provide. Even if much of this benefits society as a whole, or at least is harmless, it still does not justify the university's institutional posture of absolute neutrality.

The war in Vietnam has borne this out time and time again. The furor that has arisen on campuses over the presence of ROTC units and recruiters from manufacturers who make the weaponry of war emanates from this problem of the university's so-called neutrality. It is not neutrality; in fact it is an uncritical complicity that is not very becoming in an institution which prides itself on its critical capacities. Why must research and analysis and expertise stop short of making value judgments? The university replies that it does not stand in the way of individual researchers making such judgments. After all, it is argued, this very neutrality guarantees them that freedom. But that only begs the question, because in the end it is the university which usually gets the contract and not the individual researcher. He can say no but rarely can he stop the contract.

Furthermore, this neutrality has been deceptive in another way. Institutional decisions are really never neutral, especially when made by persons who have power. In the university this means trustees, administrators, and faculty, persons who have essentially opted for the elitist model of higher education by which education is a privilege for the qualified. Inevitably their decisions cater to the interests and needs of this privileged constituency. So it was that, for decades, no one felt it was necessary to have courses on white racism or black history or African history—not until there was a firm demand, in some instances an actual threat, by a new black constituency in the student body that these studies be included in the curriculum. For that particular constituency the university's traditional neutrality was hardly real; it was part of a racist mind-set which for years had systematically excluded them from the university on the basis that they were not qualified. All neutrality ever did was reinforce the mind-set. It opened few doors for black people.

The egalitarian model of education cannot, of course, reject the legitimacy of a kind of disciplined neutrality which holds back a final judgment and decision until all of the facts and evidence are in. But it would not absolutize neutrality as an institutional virtue. It would recognize and use the power which the university has among other institutions to affect and enable social, economic, and political change. In the end, absolute academic neutrality is a form of detachment on the part of the university which is morally irresponsible and potentially destructive of the very society it aims to serve. It is not a question of politicizing the university. The university already has political power. The real question is how the university is going to use it in interaction with other institutions and enterprises in society. The indispensability of higher education in America gives the university a unique opportunity to model intelligent and responsible institutional power which can do more to shape the character and quality and destiny of American life than any single university graduate. To recognize this and act upon it would point higher education in a radically new direction, from institutional neutrality and heightened individualism to social responsibility and community building. There is probably no other way to make it through the twentieth century.

NOTES

1. *Crisis at Columbia,* Report of the Fact-Finding Commission Appointed to Investigate the Disturbances at Columbia University in April and May 1968 (New York: Vintage Books, 1968), p. 34.

2. "Most College Trustees Found White, Protestant, Republican," *The Chronicle of Higher Education,* January 13, 1969, p. 1.

RELIGION
WITHOUT TAX BENEFITS

ELWYN A. SMITH

Is a tax exemption a "subsidy" or isn't it? That such a question takes a prominent place in determining the constitutionality of the tax-exempt status of church-owned property exhibits a new crisis of religious freedom: the United States government has such enormous fiscal power that unless certain funds connected with religion are tax-exempt the effect of its action will be hostile to religion.

The constitutionality of tax exemption is not the subject of this article; for the time being, the Supreme Court has declared it constitutional in *Walz* v. *Tax Commission* (395 U.S. 957; June 1969). We deal here with a subject not embraced in the *Walz* opinions simply because it is not the business of courts: Does religion benefit by tax-exemption privileges, or is it harmed?

Consideration of this question ordinarily stops with the horrendous question of what would happen to the institutions of religion if they were taxed. But that is not our question. Insofar as the integrity of religion is dependent upon its present institutional form, an end of institutional tax exemptions would damage religion itself. But if religion does not ultimately depend upon the sort of institutionalism familiar to Americans, then it would not necessarily be damaging to tax its institutions, however they might be reduced or altered by taxation.

This article is addressed not only to those who dispute the reasonings of *Walz* but also to those who agree with the Supreme Court that to tax the institutions of religion would be an act of hostility to religion, forbidden by the Constitution. We do not propose that the interpretation of the Constitution be made contingent upon any definition of religion. There has already been too much defining of religion by legislators, public administrators, and the courts. We are here dealing with the question of what the freedom and integrity of religion require in a society where taxation is so general, so penetrating in its effect, and so necessary.

If religion were solely a matter of an individual's attitudes and opinions, there would be little logic in religious institutions. But religion is also social: persons of common faith seek each other out; they interest themselves in issues that touch vast numbers of persons, such as problems of war and peace; they live intermixed with widely differing kinds of people; and they wish to make their decisions in the light of their religious commitments. There must be room for religion not only as attitude and opinion but also as community. The question is whether that community serves itself best by assuming the form and accepting the commitments of a corporation.

In one sense, "religion" as such has no standing in the law. A church is known to the law only as a corporation, not in terms of those spiritual bonds which draw believers into a community and induce them to support a corporation involving no financial advantage to themselves. But almost all religious groups do hold property and their religiousness in fact is not separable from their existence as a corporation. If believers should elect not to hold property they would never as a spiritual community become involved with tax problems at all. One of the central criteria of the Supreme Court in *Walz* was the minimizing of the entanglement of religion and government. While the court was not free to deny the right of religious groups to incorporate—an issue of equal protection under the law —a community of believers is entirely free to decide against incorporation. Thus the Court maintains a distance between itself and the law that maximizes religious liberty.

It is very unlikely that churches in a property-oriented culture would choose to give up their property holdings. The decision to hold property imposes limitations on the freedom of religious groups, but American churches are accustomed to those limits. Nor would a decision against the holding of property entirely dissever religion and the law. First Amendment freedoms would remain essential: the right to freedom of religious exercise, the freedom from any law establishing a religious doctrine or precept, and the right to assemble, speak, publish, and act within the bounds of the civil law without hindrance. But one thing would be resolved: the issue of whether a religious corporation should be taxed.

The religious tax issue reaches further than property tax exemption. Federal personal income tax law effectively determines the amounts of money given away by taxpayers. Furthermore, it dictates the types of corporations which survive by virtue of the government's right to determine which may receive untaxed donations. Unless a nonprofit corporation can advertise that "gifts to us are deductible under Federal Income Tax Law" it has scant chance of accumulating funds in any considerable amount. A letter from the Treasury Department informing an organization that it qualifies as a recipient of tax deductible gifts is a privilege of incalculable importance. When corporations claim the deductibility privilege on grounds that they are "religious," they subject their faith to government scrutiny. To make no such application would be a far greater security for religious freedom.

There is also the question of the exemption of income from securities and from church-owned or controlled business enterprises whose primary purpose is profit. Here is the most vulnerable aspect of ecclesiastical tax privilege. Many churches recognize that enterprises competing in the marketplace should be equally treated before the law: i.e., that church-owned businesses should pay both state and federal income and local property taxes. Should not all income produced from investments in the general economy including church investments share equally the public burden? Issues such as these, of course, arise only when the spiritual community has opted for capital accumulation. Our question is whether this is beneficial or inevitable.

There are many things that a religious community without property cannot do; the question is whether it is better or worse off relative to its purpose without property, or some kinds of it. The most obvious point touches social impact: only a paid professional leadership is capable of maintaining a large organization. American experience reveals the staggering success of this method. It has produced mass denominations, domestic and foreign missions, publishing houses, schools for clergy, and reform societies without end—against dueling (success), Sunday mails (failure); in favor of temperance (success, and then failure), schools (success, now endangered), hospitals (general success, thanks to supplementary public aid), peace (failure)—the list is long, the record impressive, if not uniformly successful. The question we raise, however, does not require judgment on the past but is a contemporaneous one. Taxation and the role of the government that taxes finance did not grow to present proportions until the Second World

War. In this new situation, does a religious community act on its social insights to best advantage through incorporation, professionalization, and massive programs?

There is nothing novel in the view that the social responsibility of a religious community is best discharged no longer by denominations, mission and education boards, and professionalized social-action groups but by the activity of the believer within the social structures themselves. As unwilling as denominations are to abandon dependence upon wealth, they have nevertheless been increasingly obliged to give their energies to training the ordinary churchman to "be a Christian on the job." The reason is obvious: most of the decision-centers in modern society cannot be reached by an ecclesiastical society.

Believers certainly should occasionally collaborate in considerable numbers for purposes of social action. We are arguing that they are no longer effective as a congeries of tax-privileged corporations. The reasons for this go far beyond tax relationships with government: particularly at fault is the professionalization of Christian vocation and the consequent alienation of members from the corporate Christian task. Churchmen are ordinarily more influenced by the ebb and flow of popular social opinion than by their clergy. The fact remains that the tax-exemption system is axiomatic to the existence of the present denominational form of the religious community. Without it, there would be an even more rapid diminishing of funds, programs, and professional services. Without tax privileges, the believer would have to assume the responsibility of his faith in the precise place in the economy where he finds himself, or be deprived of any instrument of social witness. Tax privilege is the linchpin of our surrogate system of religious responsibility.

It is fanciful to suppose that the vast accumulations of ecclesiastical wealth produced by nearly two centuries of zeal will be voluntarily dispersed, even in the best of causes, or that churches will do anything but refuse to take decisions that would further burden their wealth, no matter how great a disrepute such refusal might entail. The question is really one for the new religious communities of the future.

Should the conventicles now growing up outside the church organizations develop themselves along familiar lines—formal membership, growth, hiring professional leadership, fund-raising and property acquisition, incorporation and tax privilege? The lesson of the past has been that movements disappear unless they institutionalize, and the crux of institutionalization is paid leadership and enough wealth to control the use of property. But modern America is radically different from the early nineteenth century, when the nation had few voluntary organizations, poor communications and transportation, and little capital. Today there is instantaneous and universal communication, constant movement of people, highly developed financial structures, and national secular action societies for every cause from women's liberation to the special patriotism of the John Birch Society. There is scarcely a man of conscience who is not deluged with appeals to support reform, mostly through political action, on a scale that would have boggled Lyman Beecher. There is, in short, no lack of outlets for the social concern of believers. They need no longer form their own societies, but may act on their faith in a more diversified company. If they miss the camaraderie of their fellow believers, they are pining for the great days of nineteenth-century reform, when religious doctrine rode in tandem with reform action in highly organized and well-financed religious societies. The modern reality is that one's fellow believer can be encountered anywhere, not only in church. To the question whether there is room in the future for any sort of distinct religious community, the only answer thus far to emerge, beside the diminishing denominational structures, is the conventicle: small gatherings of the religiously concerned engaged in worshiping, reading, and teaching among themselves, discussing options for action in the general society, with little energy devoted to institutionalizing themselves. Institutionalization of benevolent activity has passed largely into the custody of the government. It is in the secular structures of government, business, and education that believers should recognize and define their responsibility. If they are not taxed it will be because in their associational life they neither possess nor desire property, not because outmoded institutions enjoy a constitutional advantage. Successful defense of the singular privilege of using ground, capital, and income that might otherwise be taxed in the general interest, as in *Walz*, may be the very face of failure.

To advocate a religious community without tax-exemption privileges is radical not so much because it would tear down existing ecclesiastical institutions and privileges— these will go the way of history, in any case—but because it would reconstitute the religious community apart from its legal recognition as religion. From the point of view of the law, a gathering of persons for religious purposes would be protected less by the first two clauses of the First Amendment and more by its latter phrases: ". . . or abridging the freedom of speech or of the press; or of the right of the people peaceably to assemble. . . ." The religion clauses of the First Amendment presuppose and necessitate at least a minimal legal definition of religion. They can only be understood as a postscript to the prolonged age of state-related Christianity from Constantine to the attenuated establishments of the modern world. Where does such phrasing point—"Congress shall make no law respecting an establishment of religion or prohibiting the free exercise thereof"—except backward, to times when such practices were condoned? So long as any society requires such a doctrine, so long as its courts face tasks of interpretation so delicate as to be characterized as a "tightrope," the language of Chief Justice Burger in *Walz,* that society is living in the shadow of religious establishment. Religion is not yet independent of the civil power in America. The principal reason for the recent erosion of "separation of church and state" is an increasing candidness about the actual intimacy of religion and public order in the United States and an utter unwillingness to accept the consequences of revered declarations of loyalty to religious liberty.

There can be only limited religious liberty so long as religious communities find it natural and inevitable to assume corporate form and accumulate property. Every such institution, whether formed for profit or not—a distinction of less importance than generally supposed—will defend its property against the encroachment of the public taxing power with whatever arguments, precedents, and means lie at hand. When the Supreme Court finds church and state less entangled under a general system of exemption, as in *Walz,* it affirms its full liberty to conclude that when and if circumstances should ever tend to entangle religion and government *because* of tax exemption the Constitution would require taxation of religious property. Such circumstances have not arisen and may not. Yet the Supreme Court has made a number of radical changes of interpretation of the Constitution as new conditions have required. In another climate, the taxing of religious property and the terminating of other exemptions might not be considered hostile to religion but a principle of equal treatment.

Resistance to any reduction of exemption privileges is built into the very form of the churches. The present religious community is above all a propertied community which will not voluntarily yield its wealth. We can conclude that only when believers themselves throw property out of the center of the religious community can they free themselves from the limitations on their effectiveness imposed by the defense of traditional privileges.

This is a society that half establishes religion. The ties that bind church and state are largely financial, whether subsidy, tax exemption, or auxiliary and indirect benefits. Those who advocate half-establishment are at pains to distinguish "subsidy" from "tax exemption." For them, the distinction is significant and necessary, but for a religious community that wishes simply to free itself from encumbrance, the obvious way is to refuse incorporation, divorce itself from tax exemption law altogether, and take social action through secular structures.

COMMUNES:
A REVOLUTIONARY ALTERNATIVE
TO INSTITUTIONAL RELIGION?

JOHN GROUTT

At the top of the stairs of a dilapidated store-front building in the East Village of New York City is a second-floor loft where a group of young people live communally. A sign reads:

> In order for the commune to survive . . .
> We ask you please don't crash here.
>
> (Sounds like extinction is well on its way.)

The last line is printed in a different color and by a different hand.

Between the lines of the sign and its talmudic comment is a striking commentary on one of the most colorful and fascinating social movements presently existing in the United States. The communal movement is growing so rapidly that it is in danger of destroying itself because of the number of young people joining the ranks daily. Those already in the communes are torn by the desire to bring as many as possible into the movement and at the same time to structure loosely a viable alternative society with very limited resources of land, food, and housing. It is a difficult task.

What the Religious Revolutionaries Are Saying

Communal groups began to appear on the West Coast and in the Southwest around 1965. At that time the new communes could be counted on one hand. Five years later no one dares hazard a guess, but the number must be in the thousands. Each month new communities are forming in every large city and on farms dotting America.

This essay will first discuss some of the difficulties in understanding the counterculture, move on to show what is religious and revolutionary about the communal movement, and finally speculate about the significance of such a major social movement vis-à-vis religion in the churches.

Why the Communal Movement Is Difficult to Understand

The exodus of young men and women from the predominant "straight" culture to the emerging counterculture and its alternate institutions and life-styles is a phenomenon already receiving attention, if for no other reason than its magnetic attraction. There has been much coverage of the communal movement by the media, complete with magazine covers in nude and living color and TV specials of mystical "Om" sessions. However, what is most striking is that the depths of this phenomenon are nearly invisible.

The "straight" society might be compared to a large ocean whose surface is familiar and where things are reasonably predictable, given the capitalistic economic system, the governmental processes that have evolved in America, and the ethical standards valued by the majority of the people in this land. But when one dips beneath the surface of that ocean a whole new world appears. Modes of operation and human interaction learned in the "straight" world cannot be depended upon to help predict or explain what occurs in the communes. As a result of new ways of perceiving reality and new patterns of living growing out of the alienation experience, there are being developed wholly new world views and alternate life-styles which are foreign to the experience of most Americans but which may point the way toward social structures of the future.

For the majority of people, the existing institutions of church, state, and family are reasonably well-structured to reflect their social interactions with others in the society. Perhaps a few reforms are needed, but the basic structures are normally unquestioned. Not so for the counterculture. It is part of a generation which refuses to accept any part of life as sacred and which is now beginning to offer the alternatives. Indeed, we shall argue that one way to understand the communal movement is to view it as a revolutionary alternative to the church and the synagogue.

But first a word of caution. When Jesus was asked why he spoke in parables, he is reported to have answered that those unfriendly to him would look without seeing and listen without hearing or understanding. The counterculture is a living parable. The result is that the most immediate problem encountered is that of understanding. Even though the words of the "straight" society and its counterpart "shadow culture"[1] often sound the same, the language games of one are not the language games of the other. The deepest experiences and resultant world views of each group are very different and the confusion which results as they meet is as humorous as it is telling. A selection of the transcript from the Chicago "Conspiracy Trial" of 1969 provides a good example:

DEFENSE ATTORNEY: Where do you reside?
ABBIE HOFFMAN: I live in *Woodstock Nation.*
DEFENSE ATTORNEY: Will you tell the court and jury where it is?
ABBIE: Yes, it is a nation of alienated young people—we carry it around with us as a state of mind, in the same way as the Sioux Indians carry the Sioux nation around with them. It is a nation dedicated to cooperation versus competition, to the idea that people should have better means of exchange than property or money, that there should be some other basis of human interaction.

> JUDGE HOFFMAN: Excuse me, sir. Read the question to the witness, please.
> STENOGRAPHER: Where do you reside?
> JUDGE HOFFMAN: Just where it is, that's all.
> ABBIE: It is in my mind, and in the minds of my brothers and sisters. It does not consist of property or of material, but rather of ideas and certain values . . .
> PROSECUTOR: This doesn't say where Woodstock Nation, whatever that is, is.
> DEFENSE ATTORNEY: Your Honor, the witness has identified it as being a state of mind and he has, I think, a right to define that state of mind.
> JUDGE HOFFMAN: No. We want the place of residence if he has one, place of doing business if you have a business, or both if you desire to tell them both. One address will be sufficent. Nothing about philosophy or India, sir, just where you live, if you have a place to live. Now you said, *Woodstock*. In what state is Woodstock?
> ABBIE: It is in the state of mind, in the mind of myself and my brothers and sisters. It is a conspiracy.[2]

Abbie Hoffman was not attempting to confuse but rather to insist that there is a revolution going on in the minds of many young people and that the usual categories of defining one's life no longer have meaning. While some ways of locating oneself in the world are dissolving, other ways are being constructed. One of these social constructs is a group living arrangement known as a commune.

It is difficult to sharply define precisely what a commune is. Robert Blair of the "Backbench," a Quaker commune in Philadelphia, describes communal living situations as a continuum from crash pads through cooperatives to intentional communities. The crash pads are usually places where people may sleep for the night ("crash") but with little or no involvement in group interaction or responsibility for the quarters. A cooperative is most often set up because it is a cheap living arrangement. An intentional community is the most highly ideological of all and is the traditional type of commune with utopian plans for the

members and usually for the society at large. In an un-
published position paper Blair writes:

> The members of this type of cooperative are attempting to
> establish in miniature a social system that will allow them to
> live as they think men should live. The motivation for a
> prophetic community is more than economic or practical, it
> is to be faithful to a religious principal, to live according to
> a life style that one believes in, to revolutionize oneself *and*
> to provide an example for a revolutionary society.

While these distinctions between the three types of
group living situations appear clear-cut on paper, the real-
life situation shifts back and forth among them. Here new
family arrangements are replacing the nuclear family as
both space and time relationships are constantly being re-
negotiated in a world where there are few givens. The
ecology of personal inner space and interpersonal outer
space is being explored within the supportive community
of the commune and new forms of socialization are being
tried for size. Indeed, much of the excitement experienced
by people living communally is found in the freedom to
probe the unknown for new forms of human interrelated-
ness and community.

What Is Religious about the Communal Movement?

A recurrent theme in the hippie counterculture is that
we are at the dawning of a new age, the age of Aquarius.
The Piscean Age (Pisces is the twelfth sign of the zodiac
when the stellar constellation resembles a fish) was the
age of Christianity. It was an age of reason and has now
run its course in the nearly two thousand years since
its beginning, culminating in the technological society.

A new astrological age has begun to emerge. In the
Aquarian age, a new consciousness will mark the experience of men. One of its signs will be men and women living in close communities with as much sharing as possible

101

both in material goods and human relationships. There will be more reliance on feeling, intuition, and the dreams of men. It is a deeply romantic world view, not a rationalistic one.

In order to understand this culture one must grasp the centrality of this sense of newness. New wine cannot be put into old wineskins. They will not hold. Neither will old modes of perception be sufficient to understand the new consciousness. Already we have transgressed this warning by attempting to classify the communal movement as religious. Yet given our present limitation of language this seems one of the most descriptive terms we have at present.

Certainly what constitutes "religion" is a much discussed question among scholars and religious men. Can drugs lead to genuine religious experience or are they counterfeit? Are mystical experiences or adherence to creedal formulas the most important elements of religion? Must religion to be legitimate be found within church structures, or is it more authentic in the lone individual seeking his God? Can atheistic Buddhism be considered religion or must one hold to a personal God?

Rather than become entangled in this perplexing set of problems, we shall simply note that many of the experiences, ideas, myths, and practices commonly labeled "religious" appear central in the communal experience. The total constellation of these elements within this social movement leads to the conclusion that American society is indeed faced with an important religious phenomenon. What now are some of these elements?

Story and Myth. Since reason falls short of the dreams and hopes of many men the highest ideals and deepest experiences have repeatedly been enshrined in the forms of story and myth. Here, on the edge of human experience, the use of myth and story enables one to pass back and forth into the mysterious without sharp logical distinctions or clearly formulated concepts. By their use, man is taken beyond reason into mystery and hope. Often this expresses more about existence than any scientific or creedal statement. Religious language in general has been far more prescriptive than descriptive. "God is love" does less to describe God than to say how man wants to walk forward in life. Stories and myth add another dimension by placing this in an existential setting.

Further, it is in the religious myths and stories that societies tell themselves that they make sense of their world. Here the highest level of legitimation takes place and man explains to himself the *total* gestalt or configuration of his cosmos. Here too, mystery, awe, and the incomprehensible serve as the ground for all lesser existence.

The stories which enshrine the religious ideals of today's hip youth are being expanded from the traditional Western Judeo-Christian biblical writings alone to include the *I Ching,* Vedantic scriptures, Zen insights and practices, astrological books, American Indian lore, modern fiction and poetry, especially that pertaining to the drug experiences (e.g., *The Visions of Don Juan, A Yaqui Way of Knowledge,* and the novels of Herman Hesse) and communal living (e.g., *The Harrard Experiment, Walden II*) and manuals on organic gardening and foods. All these blend in a constantly shifting and enlarging set of scriptures which are frequently supplemented by private revelation experienced in some form by a group. This may take the form of messages given a member while he is in a trance; or, for the more revolutionary, action-oriented groups, simply a decision arrived at in a group meeting.

Closely connected with this is the ideal of "voluntary primitivism" (as Lou Gottlieb, one of the foremost theoreticians of the movement, calls it) which marks those embracing it. Thus in many groups there is great interest in American Indian lore (including the Peyote sacrament of the Neo-American church), clothing reminiscent of the

What the Religious Revolutionaries Are Saying

American pioneers, body hair which seems to grow longer as each year of the movement passes, nudity taken as casually as clothing, belief in reincarnation which bonds men into a line of the race, ritual in the form of rock music and drug communion, Shaker-type dances which bring the participant to the edge of ecstasy, group praying with mantras (OM is the most popular) which give the feeling of blending into the Eternal, and a deep belief in the laws of Karma operating to insure a cosmic justice.

Commitment to this way of life is often very deep for most of the members. Typically the age of commune members is somewhere in the twenties, and many have given up careers which they were quite capable of pursuing within the system. In its earlier years the movement seemed to attract many high-school and college drop-outs, but recent converts include large numbers of college graduates and successful professional people with no profession unrepresented.

In order to enter the commune these people usually give up all personal property and the security it provides. The property has either been sold or brought to the commune for the use of all, and this often allows the commune to increase its own capital resources or to maintain itself. As a result, few remain long on the edge without being quickly drawn in as full-fledged members with deep personal commitments to the movement.

Loyalty is often more to the movement rather than to a particular commune. The furniture in one commune often originally belonged to persons who now live elsewhere. Property may be bought with a down-payment and payments will be made by the members who happen to be there when they come due. One of the earliest communes, Drop City in Trinidad, Colorado, is legally incorporated with a president named John Fudge and a board of directors which includes Peter Rabbit. If they ever existed these people no longer live at Drop City and none of the original and imaginative builders of its famous geodesic dome living-structures are there any longer. Payments are still met each year by a constantly shifting membership.

The significance of this pattern is striking. The question of private property is one of the first issues raised by this new life-style. "No trespassing" signs are of the old order. The history of many religious movements reveals similar behavior; for example, the account given in Acts 4:32 where "no one said that any of the things which he possessed was his own, but they had everything in common." Medieval monasticism and the nineteenth-century religious communities in North America practiced similar communal ownership. The spirit of tribal ownership known to primitive societies and many radical religious movements is stirring in a land where capitalism and private ownership presently are blessed by the established religions.

When the principle "from each according to his ability, to each according to his needs" is operative, one way of life necessarily replaces another. As trust in personal property disappears, trust in the goodness of people is to replace it. The ideal of "open land" is popular with many rural groups. This means that land may be used by anyone who wishes to live or farm there. When they leave it is open to anyone else. At present, these areas are usually owned by one person who was wealthy enough to purchase it and declare it open. More and more these owners seem to want to "deed it to God" or set up some sort of legal fiction which will show that no one owns the land and that it is for the use of any who need it.

A Sense of Power over Cosmic Events. A feeling of control over man's destiny is part of this movement. This divides the communes into two groups: those committed to political or revolutionary change, and those more interested in developing inner life. We shall discuss this again as we inquire into the revolutionary aspects of the movement, but for the moment we are trying to understand whether *both* branches might be considered religious.

What the Religious Revolutionaries Are Saying

Revolutionary tactics are studied by groups desiring to change the external world. Others delve deeply into the inner world of personal experience and seek religious models suited to describe their experience. Both groups are included in "the movement," but it is often difficult to reconcile a religiously orientated commune with a revolutionary one unless both can be understood as power language, one in relation to outer space (social structures) and the other in relation to inner space (psychic experience).

One important aspect of religion is a sense of one's ability to persuade the deity, one's power over cosmic events resulting from prayers or actions. On this basis, the communal movement in both revolutionary and religious forms may be considered religious. Both groups are trying to reformulate myths and ideologies (as well as life-styles) which will allow man to understand the forces that shape his inner and outer destiny, while at the same time trying to gain some control over irrational forces which help shape their lives. That religion has always been concerned with these forces is shown by stories and myths that seek to explain the mysterious. It seems clear that American society is indeed faced with a social movement containing many important religious elements.

Freedom. If one theologizes in terms of liberty, then again the communes are very religious. The key event in the Hebrew Bible was the freeing of Israel from slavery; the greatest achievement of Jesus was the freeing of believers from the tyranny of death. The Protestant Reformation was, in part, a social reflection of a new awareness of personal freedom accompanying the breakdown of the authoritarian feudal system. This theological model of liberation is impossible to ignore.

Today the word *liberation* is used in place of *salvation,* but the same reality remains. The "salvific communities" known as churches are being replaced by "liberated zones" known to many of today's youth as "communes." The sense of liberation that men have felt in the most memorable events of religious history is an essential element of social religious experience. The present movement offers that excitement to many, and if it continues to ignite imaginations it may rank with the Exodus, the Resurrection, and the Reformation as the crucial event in the religious experience of its devotees.

Holy Poverty. Part of the present phenomenon was described by one young man as that of "Dharma Bums," that is, religious pilgrims begging for sustenance. This is a holy tradition of the East and one that was once well-known in the West in the form of penitents and orders of begging monks and nuns. When it reappears in the form of free food stamps and the street-corner greeting, "Got any spare change, brother?" it causes consternation to a work-oriented society. It might remind us that mendicancy has returned and that there might be something more valuable than production.

The "straight" world is greatly disturbed by all this because it senses what might be the death pangs of its own life-style just as the Roman Empire feared for its life when confronting the emerging Christian church. It is clear that this is a critical struggle of values between the ruling classes and those who reject it.

Search. Another feature of this emerging life-style is its nomadic nature. The theme of wandering and search has been important in the religious history of man. In the communes ad hoc social relationships seem to border on the superficial as groups are constantly being formed and promptly dissolved when they no longer fulfill significant functions for their members. Revolutionary communes form and dissolve, and new ones take form around need for new action. Friends regroup as they feel they have outgrown a particular family arrangement. New members come and old ones go as the gestalt repatterns itself. The ancient Israelites were a people in search of a land; the present generation is a people in search of community.

Metanoia à la LSD. The hippie culture would not be what it is today without the drug explosion of the mid sixties. Many of those who use drugs heavily say that they have attained states of consciousness unfamiliar to most people in the West until recently. Work being done with LSD therapy in Europe and at one center in the United States seems to confirm this.

A Czechoslovakian psychotherapist, Stanislav Grof, presently at Spring Grove in Maryland, classifies material brought to the surface in LSD therapy in three stages: Freudian, Rankian, and Jungian. In the first phase of therapy much of the psychic material uncovered by Freud surfaces in the patient in the form of guilt feelings, sexual problems, and authority difficulties. In the second stage existential questions about the meaning of life arise. Near the end the person undergoes an "ego-death" wherein the individual experiences the dissolution of his separated ego and blends into the cosmic experience. Finally, there occurs what Grof labels as the Jungian phase with material centering around cosmic awareness, unity with the cosmos, the white light, experience of the All, peace and brotherhood. What we are seeing in the communes is an attempt to structure this inner experience into a social existential life-style which reflects it. Intense group living and sharing is a natural development.

Among American psychologists Jung has not been popular. If this movement is any indication, we should see a Jungian revival, since Jung's models best reflect the altered consciousness of drug culture.

Toward a Hip Theology. From the point of view of theology new models must be found to appraise this movement. Rational theological speculation is irrelevant and dead for these people. Call it a return to pietism, fundamentalism, or mysticism—it does not matter. It is all of these, but much more. While hip religion often originates in a chemically induced state, it goes beyond that. A meta-noia occurs wherein lives are dramatically altered, insights permanently gained, experiences traumatic. Meditation without drugs often continues. "Natural highs" from grooving on nature, music, and people are another common result; a lasting appreciation of the beauty of life and death is another. All of these are reminiscent of the mystical experiences of saints and holy men, and it is difficult if not impossible to distinguish the altered lives of many members of this movement from that of some mystics.

Toward an Image of Man. From all this a new image of man emerges. There is great trust in the innate goodness of man. He is communal and social and the needs of others are recognized and function as voluntary limiting mechanisms in human interaction in place of laws and regulations. This is labeled "anarchy" by the "straight" world.

Those who belong to the movement see us all as on "spaceship earth," needing one another to survive. National boundaries, church memberships, social classes, and skin colors disappear before this experience. Creation is united; all is one. Man blends with the cosmos. Man is God, and God is man. There is tremendous respect for diversity, and each person must be permitted, even encouraged, to do his own thing. There are obvious problems with this, but the ideal is to convert the other person to see this. Then individual selfishness will disappear.

Growth of the individual is of great concern in this image of man. Experience of an expanding consciousness is central. Man is seen in terms of process rather than as a static model with distinct elements which fragment him into alienated parts. The whole man rejoices in both sensuality and asceticism. Fasting is as important as organic food for the cleansing of the body and spirit. The proper breathing taught by Kundalini yoga is as important as the path of work taught by Karma yoga. Yet, while this is basically a holistic view of the human experience, heavy emphasis on the spiritual makes it tend toward a new Platonism. Ready-made blueprints provide the plan for the ideal individual living in Utopia. This issue is yet to be faced by the movement.

How Can This Movement Be
Considered Revolutionary?

There is debate today among the philosophers of the communal movement concerning whether certain aspects of the movement are not actually counterrevolutionary. Are not the groups which form "extended families" and experience drug-induced highs really fostering a false consciousness and diverting energy from revolutionary activity?

The polarization between introverted groups trying to develop interpersonal relationships and extroverted groups interested in changing social structures through direct action is evident. Rick Margolies calls it the "wheelie-feelie polarization."

> The wheelies are the politicos, the wheeler-dealers of our movement with a background in history, economics, and politics, and consequently see most of the movement's concern in structural and programmatic ways. The feelies are the artists of the movement who are into art, dancing, music, the occult, the mystical, the various schools of psychology, and thus see most of the movement's concerns in psychodramatic terms of people being more gentle and expressive with each other.[3]

Those engaged in revolutionary and political activity criticize the "feelies" as the cop-outs of the movement. They see them as living with false consciousness about the true nature of social reality because they are tied up with their own individual or small-group consciousness. They are not aware of the powerful but hidden forces in the society which control them. The "wheelies" would confront such things as the military-industrial complex and existing political institutions with group political or revolutionary activity. Nothing short of an overthrow of the present power structures will accomplish that, they argue.

Many in the nonpolitical communes disagree. They see themselves as truly revolutionary, for their very life-style is revolutionary at a fundamental level. We live a fractionated existence where man is indeed alienated from his world. Work and family are two isolated spheres. School has less and less to do with life's deepest experiences and has become more of a training ground for the values and slots of the establishment. Play is blocked off into weekends while self-development is relegated to the few moments of spare time.

Persons within the communal movement envision it as a way to integrate man and his world once again. No longer will life be broken into segments having little connection with each other. Man will see, feel, smell, and taste the satisfaction of his work. The home will be a place where total living takes place, including work, learning, play, love-making, eating, and prayer. The need for the hard goods of modern technology will be reduced to a minimum because these often act as the instruments of alienation. One result of this is of course a drastic reduction in spending, which will not do much to raise the gross national product, so important for a capitalistic system. Thus, by providing an environment which counteracts alienation and encourages fully integrated human beings, the communal movement is undermining the greater society which depends for its existence on alienated man. The success of the movement means the destruction of present social institutions.

However, the revolutionary power of the movement goes further. By ignoring as many of the power structure's institutions as possible, it is setting up a wholly new, alternative society. This is being done quietly but the movement believes it will accomplish more in this way than by using direct political action or violence to try to bring down the existing structures. So, their scheme establishes alternatives: the communal family in place of the nuclear family; free schools in place of academia; voluntary primitivism in place of technology; food conspiracies in place of capitalistic retailing; religious experience in place of institutional churches; anarchy in place of government; aquarian consciousness replacing piscean; a constellation of integrated work-pleasure in place of the job/leisure dichotomy; organic rather than chemically treated foods; open land in place of private property.

This life-style is obviously radically different from that of the majority of Americans. The argument of the "feelies" is that if enough people adopt it the establishment will crumble. The revolution will have occurred within the hearts and lives of men; structures will emerge to reflect that. People now living communally are the harbingers of the new consciousness.

Whether one agrees with this reasoning or not, history provides many such examples of utopian hopes which have succeeded in changing the course of events. Christianity itself, the monastic movement, the Mormons, and the Marxian utopia have affected the world we now live in. There are enough serious and dedicated men and women in this movement to see it through several decades of probing for viable alternatives.

The Significance of This for Institutional Religion

What is one to make of all this? While the forms, values, and institutions erected by one society seem to be crumbling, another society is struggling to emerge. One still holds the reins of power and money, the other ignores it and claims it can succeed without either. The countersociety has already begun to emerge.

One thing that is clear is that the canopies which

legitimated a "unified American society" and institutional religion no longer serve that purpose. The realities of the greater society are no longer the subjective world of many young people. Whereas the present power structures reflect the objectification of the subjective experience of the "straight" society, in the communes the counterculture is objectifying its own subjective experience.

The new myths and utopian ideologies are the new culture's expression of its legitimating power and its source of inspiration. Communes display publicly a new *Weltanschauung.*

The Age of Aquarius is the new culture's reformation. Older forms of community presently existing in church and synagogue and the Catholic religious orders of priests and nuns are diminishing as their relevance fails; membership in communes is increasing almost geometrically. Men and women are still seeking group living and community, but in forms which better reflect their experience of the world and their protest against it.

NOTES

1. The British "shadow cabinet" consists of the experts in the party out of power who sit opposite the government party in Parliament. They are the constant critics of the government, working for its downfall and prepared to step in with alternative political solutions if the government should fall. So, too, the "shadow culture" sees itself ever ready to step in when the present social structures fall. It is beginning to prepare a complete alternative society as we shall see. I am indebted to Professor George Hicks at Brown University for this analogy.

2. *The United States v. David T. Dellinger,* Microfilm edition (Chicago: Commercial Clearing House), reel 5, pp. 12399–12401. The court testimony was given December 23, 1969.

3. Rick Margolies, "On Community Building," in *The New Left: A Collection of Essays,* ed. Priscilla Long (Boston: P. Sargent, 1969), pp. 363-64. This quotation is from a revised and edited version appearing in *Currier* (Georgetown University), 18 (May 1970): 63.

PSYCHEDELIC DRUGS
AND THE AMERICAN
RELIGIOUS EXPERIENCE

A. THEODORE KACHEL

Psychedelic drugs, to be properly understood, must be viewed in the context of America's general drug usage. Even excluding the great number of prescription and nonprescription drugs that do not alter subjective state or mood, there remains a vast array of substances used daily by the majority of Americans that do alter their perceptions of reality and sense of self. These substances, all of which in some way alter the subjective state, include everything from aspirin to LSD. There is caffeine in our coke and our coffee, stimulating acids in the teas we drink; there is nicotine in the cigarettes we smoke, and countless alcoholic substances to drink. There are sedatives used to help us sleep. There is a variety of amphetamines and barbiturates to speed up our basic metabolic process. These last two drugs are only available on prescription, but this does not stop their widespread distribution in our society, both legally and illegally. There is also a variety of widely advertised mood-altering substances sold without prescription, including No Doz, Compoz, ViVarin, Nytol, Sleepeze, etc. And tranquilizers are prescribed by doctors for millions of Americans.

The use of chemical substances to alter subjective states is learned at mother's knee. Psychedelic drug usage is different, but not so much so when viewed against this kind of pervasive drug-using background. In the development of a drug technology we have tried to find a substance to deal with almost any problem. One might say that the technological "trap" in drug usage among many Americans is the belief that pills will solve problems.

It is realistic to predict that within the next twenty-five years, as a result of pharmaceutical research and development, we will have a drug technology that will enable us with a high degree of precision to achieve any subjective state we wish. On the basis both of this development and some trends already present in the treatment of mentally-ill patients, it is easy to foresee that the use of such substances may not be left to the individual; rather, others may use drugs to manage the subjective state of individuals or whole segments of the population. Just recently through a controversy in Omaha, Nebraska, it was brought to light that some doctors in cooperation with school officials had prescribed tranquilizing drugs for certain students who were considered unmanageable in the classroom. This tendency toward handling "problem people" through the use of drugs has great potential to change drug abuse from a personal into a social problem. The issue then will be *who* shall do the controlling. Under what circumstances will doctors, school officials, or other public servants deem it wise to manage segments of the population through the manipulation of their subjective states? Many university regents and their administrative staffs may be tempted to deal with campus unrest through such sophisticated control of the subjective states of unruly students.

These general developments are not unrelated to the use of psychedelic drugs today by a significant number of young people. Humorous members of the hip communities have co-opted a famous chemical industry's slogan, "Better living through better chemistry," as their life-style. That slogan when placed in the context of the growth and refinement of drug technology has both a heartening and a chilling effect. Mood-altering substances place in man's hand the ability to alter his subjectivity. By means of these drugs, technological reason with its models of rationality, manipulation, and control of process can now be applied to the inside of man himself. In this development we have a "technologizing" of the human spirit itself. Man has managed finally to reach into his interior most private self and find a technological way to manipulate this last frontier. Subjectivity can now be objectified, made public, and brought under discreet control to serve the social purposes of society and the needs and interests of those persons in positions of control. This seems to continue the pervasive trend of technology to externalize functions initially present in man into repeated processes. Such repeatability is the essence of a machine. The drug technology could be used to reduce the subjectivity of man to mechanical processes.

One of the basic models of technological production is that man produces products which he then consumes. Man creates things that are to be related to his personal biochemical system through various kinds of usages or absorption processes; he reprocesses what he himself mechanically produced. This consumer model of relating to productivity is applicable to drug technology. In other words, we create machines to build synthetic or organic chemicals. These machines produce the products in massive amounts and then we market them through advertising and public marketing. These products are then consumed or reprocessed through the individual's biological system. With respect to drugs this is literally and physically the case since one has to take the drug into one's body and let it directly affect the organism.

As a general model, one can broaden the concept of consumption to include use of various products through mental absorption or as physical extensions of the human body. In this we have a feedback process. We create products, we market these products to ourselves, and we consume these products. There is a sense in which this technological view of society and the consumption model for how human beings as individuals relate to this society has grown to nearly absolute dominance in the American social system. There are not many options in the society in which one does anything but consume as an individual isolated self. This is true not only in terms of hardware or material productivity but also in terms of cultural productivity in the arts or religion, or knowledge in general. This cycle necessarily produces alienation, i.e., a subjective separation between the using self and his created products, a sense of distance or otherness between one's productivity and one's self. The products exist as objects over against us, and the only way that the subjective self is deemed meaningful is by its ability to consume these other objects. A general class of psychoactive drugs could be used to reduce individuals to mechanized products to be consumed socially by other persons' usage. Such consumption would be cultural cannibalism.

Psychedelic drugs fit directly into this pattern until the last stage. At that point the psychedelic experience, because of what it does to the subjectivity of man, tends to reverse the technological process and become in its basic subjectivity, antitechnological. The clinical and biochemical studies of the brain that have been done with the high-energy psychedelics such as LSD, Mescaline, and Pilocybin are still incomplete. We do not understand precisely how these drugs affect the metabolic processes and change the brain chemistry to produce their peculiar subjective state. The experience, however, can at least be clinically described. I believe it is adequate, however, to describe the process as a temporary reduction of the automatic or subconscious filtration processes of the brain in relationship to the sensory input in the environment and to the memory's recall of events.

Psychologists have known for years that we learn at a very early age to see, to feel, to think, to order even sensory experience in a certain way. Part of this is determined by our innate biological capacities, part by the emotional context of our early years, part by the natural environment. This subconscious filtering of sensation so that certain input is considered more important and highlighted, while other data is reduced or ignored, gives a priority structure to the basic reality that the brain uses at its conscious decision-making levels. High energy psychedelics such as LSD seem temporarily to reduce or remove this primal ordering process of the brain so that all sensory input or remembered past experience is equally present and/or equally valued. This explains some of the stimulus-bound situations in which a person on LSD might sit and stare for some time at a simple inanimate object, such as a chair, or a doorknob, or a particular drawer handle. This is equally true for events or emotional experiences recalled from memory into a present reliving of that reality. There is a sense in which both present sensory input or remembered states are now experienced freshly in a way that is *unmediated* by any prior subconscious ordering of reality. In certain persons such a subjective state obviously produces a chaotic sense which sociologists might call "anomie," i.e., complete orderlessness, while in other subjects it produces an interpenetration of self in unity or equality with all being. Some psychiatrists have seen this chaotic side of the state as a model of the psychotic experience. Other men have valued the positive subjective interpretation of the psychedelic experience as an analogue to religious or mystical experience.

Whatever interpretation or variety of interpretations is placed on the psychedelic state, it is phenomenologically adequate to say that it is a subjective state in which the self *feels* itself to be an organic part of the cosmos. It is no longer alienated or separate from the organic living whole of the universe. Individuals may interpret such a subjective state as either heaven or hell or some middle ground in between those extremes. But a phenomenological assessment of their reports, together with what we presently understand of the brain chemistry in relationship to this experience, does suggest a loss of self-boundaries and a sense of unity with reality. It is as if the self had the whole universe as its subjective personality state. No longer is there an inside to one's personality and an outside, an objective reality to which one is relating; rather, all is one subjective lived reality.

Psychedelic drugs have turned against the basic subjective consciousness created by the technological process, contradicting this alienated state through an overwhelming experience of enlarged unified subjectivity. In technology man has created a process in which he increasingly runs himself from outside of himself; in the psychedelic experience this relationship is reversed so that one subjectively experiences the self from the inside in relation to the outside of reality. There is no longer a split; the inside and the outside are one. It is ironic that synthetic and organic drugs developed through technological processes now turn and give lie to the basic technological state of meaning. If one values positively this psychedelic state it is easy to see how one might organize one's life and efforts in opposition to the externalizing tendencies of modern society. To put this positively, people would begin to develop ways of relating to the actual productivity of their hands and minds with a higher sense of personal worth; this is in contrast to the pattern whereby meaning is added to the self through consumption. A look at hip culture confirms such a reversal in life-style and in artistic and craftlike working-patterns.

What the Religious Revolutionaries Are Saying

Psychedelic substances have been available to man from the dawn of creation but have not at all times been used in primarily religious ways. They have also been widely distributed geographically and historically. In relationship to man's development of his consciousness they tend to come and go. My own research into the relationship of psychedelic drugs and religious experience has led me to conclude that they occur in three instances. First they may be used early in the development of a particular ancient civilization—for example, soma among the Indians in Southeast Asia and peyote and the sacred mushroom among the Central American peoples. A second cultural situation in which psychedelic drugs are found in relation to religion is in contemporary nonliterate tribal societies. This is the case in Latin America today where tribes use psychedelic snuffs. The third situation in which psychedelic drugs tend to be related to religion is after a major crisis in which a culture has lost its sense of meaning. This is particularly true when a culture is overwhelmed by outside invaders. The best documented example of such a usage of psychedelic drugs is the emergence of the peyote religion among the native American peoples in the United States in the late nineteenth century.

In each of these three situations it is easy to surmise that the drug is used to produce a surge of activity in the basic subjectivity of a communal sense of meaning. These substances, in effect, increase the amount of subjective energy available to the community in its search for common meaning. In high dosages they may in fact provide a subjective way of overcoming the present or older meaning system and a way of randomly moving toward new images, myths, or cultural themes which can be elaborated as new sources for communal meaning. This occurs at a time when the issues of material productivity seem to take second place to the issue of human meaningfulness.

Psychedelic Drugs

Why then the markedly increased use of psychedelic drugs among the young and the intellectuals in the United States shortly after the beginning of the 1960s? Our discussion of the subjective experience of technological society suggests that at least one of the causes is the location of worth, value, and meaning in external and alienated products that must be consumed. This decreases the individual's ability to create and sustain his own meaning. He is increasingly dependent upon the marketing system and his ability to participate in that system if he is to sustain a sense of personal worth. In any society an individual is dependent upon the community and its mechanisms for the sustenance of his meaning system. In the modern technological society the ratio between the ability to sustain one's sense of worth out of personal activity and one's need for the community to confer meaning on him is shifted increasingly to favor communal marketing mechanisms. This might be seen as one of the basic sources for the general discussion about alienation occurring today in America. Alienation, however, is not new to American society even in this century. Technological alienation may be increasingly the case, but a single social factor seldom provides adequate explanation for the development of any movement. The rise of psychedelic drug usage in American society in the early sixties is certainly not reducible to just the alienating subjective effects of a growing technological society. This is but one of the social factors involved.

Another factor that might be related to this economic one is the growth of population and its intensification through urban migration in the cities during and after World War II. Again, this was not the only social factor, but it is an interesting one to examine. Americans feel crowded. It seems to be historically true that the kinds of people that have settled in America do not like to be crowded. Perhaps the great attraction for early immigration to North America was the space provided for expansion. Many historians and social scientists have commented about the subjective importance of the western frontier. There was almost limitless space in which one might settle, or so it seemed to the early European settlers. A common and continuing theme in American experience, therefore, has been that if you do not like the way things are here, move on over the hill, out into the spacious frontier, where you will have room to "do your own thing." No matter how we may evaluate this way of dealing with conflict among people, it is an old and hallowed tradition in America. In American religious tradition the biblical metaphor of the "promised land" was quite often used in respect to the promise of the frontier space in America society. This understanding of space is one of the basic mythological structures in which American religious experience and our subjective sense of self has developed.

After World War II, with the sudden growth in family size and the migration to the city, an individual could no longer go to the frontier and find more room. There was no more space. There were people everywhere. In the early sixties there was a quest for new vision. It is not surprising that John F. Kennedy named his call to the American people "the New Frontier." Space had been our safety valve. It had been our way of dealing with social conflict or, in truth, of not dealing with it. When that safety valve was no longer available we began self-consciously to be aware of our differences and our conflicting self-interests. So the social problems of the 1960s emerged as the ever present context of political and social conflict.

Psychedelic drugs had really been available in synthetic form since the late 1940s. Much experimentation had gone on among clinical doctors and some psycho-pharmacologists during the 1950s. By the end of the 1950s interest had waned, as exhibited by the decline in research studies. Given the hunger for space and the American sense that such a quest was an honored and hallowed one, it should not be surprising that Timothy Leary and Richard Alpert, through their psychedelic experiments at Harvard, were seen as opening a new frontier. To this spacious frontier flocked many young people and many intellectuals, since they perhaps most of all experienced alienation and frustration in dealing with the social problems of the cities. This was their way of moving on. It was a way, at least in the initial stages, of avoiding conflict by hoping that all people might cross this frontier and find in the psychedelic experience inner space to overcome the loss of outer space. Through the discovery of this inner space many early users hoped that the conflict and social problems that technological society had produced through its externalizing processes would become insignificant in the light of the spiritual richness and possibilities of man's own inner self. Early psychedelic users, therefore, were evangelistic in their proclamation of the drug's potentials. Until LSD was made federally illegal in late 1966, the psychedelic movement had much about it of the quality of an early frontier revival. Mass meetings, human be-ins, and love-ins all harked back to the traditions of the revivalistic camp meetings of the earlier frontier.

If space was an important mythological reality in the American consciousness, revivialism as the social form of this new religiosity also pointed to another theme. Americans have long believed in equal accessibility of all men to the saving experience. This, of course, is the egalitarianism of American society as worked out in American religion. Whatever sense of salvation a religion might offer to the people of America, it had to be one equally available to the lowest and to the highest. There was a leveling sought in all American churches and synagogues. Certainly there have been movements and churches that tried to stand against this for a variety of theological and even class reasons, but the popular religious movements that spread across America during its early formation were predominantly egalitarian movements. The presence, then, of a synthetic drug that could produce this powerful subjective experience was equally available to all persons regardless of what he or she may have been before taking the drug. This new religious charisma fit precisely into the American tradition of religious egalitarianism and revivalistic fervor. Psychedelic drugs open the vastness of inner space to all who use them, whereas the exploration of extraterrestrial space by NASA opened no new general frontier to catch the individual's spirit since it was limited to only the few astronauts.

If the psychedelic drug provided a reversal to the technological experience of American society it also had in its religious impact a similar cultural reversal. Another emerging theme in American experience has been the progressive secularization of religion in American society. This was a particular kind of secularization, as Martin Marty has recently argued. It was not the antireligious fervor of the continental religious revolutions, nor was it the "mere secularity" of the British Isles with their benign tolerance of religious differences. It was instead a secularization that was in fact a form of religious change. The traditions that came to America from Europe and Britain underwent a subjective shift and reordering of their religious priorities. Two of these themes we have already talked about and related to the emerging drug religiosity—the myth of space and the demand for experiential equality. The theme of secularization is primarily illuminated when one observes the unbelievable institutional and organizational efforts expended through voluntary associations which mark the pattern of American religious communal life. Herein the technological process of externalization was having its impact upon American religiosity. Through the efforts to organize and bring everyone into a voluntary religious association externalization of the religious community took place. The religious fervor and piety that developed a total life-style on the frontier moved in the late nineteenth and early twentieth century into a style that has been described as "churchianity." Religious experience was reduced and replaced by consumable religious products. You had to belong to a church in order to participate in the production of religious products and in their consumption through institutional communities. This is a shift away from individual experience and the human self toward institutional life and technology.

Religion, as secularized by Americans in the diverse Judeo-Christian traditions, was to serve a purpose in one's life. Religion became functional. It taught children certain moral values. It provided a pause for spiritual refreshment at a given time and at a given place. It was only as good as it was able functionally to fulfill certain needs to consume religious products. Even revivalism became more of a packaged touring religious entertainment show. Revivals no longer sought personal transformation, despite their continuing rhetoric, but rather sought to draw in church members and in their follow-up afterwards to return church people to the institutional structures.

The psychedelic experience with its subjective experience in which the self becomes a feeling part of the universal whole, flew in the face of the carefully compartmentalized and institutionalized religion that had come into being through the twentieth-century secularization of religion in the United States. It jumped back over the churches to American revivalistic experience. Drug experience was taken as a way out of secularized religion toward a new commitment to the creation of a total life-style. The hippies became the new pietists by ordering their total existence in relationship to the primary importance of their basic religious experience. That basic religious experience is the subjective sense of oneness with the compassionate universal reality. It is not surprising that the generally privatized and externalized religions of America did not make sense to the drug culture's religious experience. Their religious experience was total in the sense that it gave them a subjective sense of being one with the world. The hip communities rejected consumerism. They had no use for using or absorbing alienated products produced by massive mechanical systems; they rather sought to return to the fundamentals of life. In some cases they returned to an agricultural existence in isolated rural communities. In all cases they reorganized their total life-style, with particular attention to their diet, their way of dress, their search for simplicity and purity. They represent indeed a new flourishing pietism in the American religious experience.

After an early revivalistic phase for which they were generally ridiculed, ignored, or persecuted by their middle-class parents, the mass media, and other official members of the American system, the hip communities withdrew into communal monastic existence. Because of this withdrawal many commentators have assumed the hippies are dead or disappearing. Will they survive? There is much about the simplicity of their life-style that suggests the human race starting out all over again. They are reinventing patterns of religion, the family, marriage, diet—all at a basic and simple level. They are not unsophisticated: they are rather concentrating on the essentials so that what they see as humanly significant stands out with stark boldness in contrast to the American social landscape. Lewis Mumford refers to them as persons who live as if the nuclear bomb had already dropped. Perhaps we should see them as postapocalyptic. Unlike the early Christians the end is not coming but has already come, so they have started again.

From what I have said about technology and its basic externalizing process, the real question is whether, if we reject the prophetic word of the psychedelic peoples, American society will survive. Will modern American mankind prevail? The psychedelic drug is only one element of the crisis of our times—perhaps it is a key experiential referent for determining the nature of the spiritual crisis we face. Certainly it is not a pill to solve our cultural problems. Rather, the psychedelic experience is a parable to be listened to by a technological culture which seems bent on gaining the whole world and in the process losing its soul.

ABORTION AND THE
THEOLOGICAL ENDEAVOR

STEPHEN S. DIXON

Creative theology has never been a static discipline dealing with unchanging principles. The cutting edge of Christian theology is tested by its ability to explore and illuminate man's ongoing present and past in such a way that God's reconciling love can be experienced as a life-giving guide for the future. Any redeeming encounter with God carries with it a necessary criticism of one's self, one's tradition, and one's present and future possibilities. As a rocket aimed at a moving target, so must theology constantly correct its course.

In this light the Bible can be seen as a diachronical self-criticism of Israel. This criticism was capable of apparently contradicting the most solid theological basis of the past in order to maintain a proper orientation in a changed time. Perhaps the most marked example of this can be seen in the Ten Commandments: "I the Lord your God am a jealous God, visiting the iniquity of the fathers upon the children to the third and the fourth generation . . ." (Exod. 20:5). When this was used to shirk moral responsibility, Ezekiel (18:2-4) had to correct the course in order to maintain a proper orientation:

What do you mean by repeating this proverb concerning the land of Israel, "The fathers have eaten sour grapes, and the children's teeth are set on edge"? As I live, says the Lord God, this proverb shall no more be used by you in Israel. Behold, all souls are mine; the soul of the father as well as the soul of the son is mine: the soul that sins shall die.

Whenever theological statements shield man from his responsibility, they no longer give the proper orientation and must therefore be discarded.

The history of medical ethics manifests many examples of this problem. Modern science and technology have brought about a revolution in man's control over nature. The models offered for dealing with this situation are evolution and revolution. We know, however, that although the evolutionary steps were of some historical advantage for the propagation of an individual species, they were by no means the only possible or even the best steps for that species. Indeed, the chance steps of our phylogenetic history were neither consciously made nor consciously controlled. As such they give us no sound basis for corporate or personal ethical decisions which must be aware of contingency as well as of continuity in all aspects of life history. Ethical decisions will be molded by the past, but they must be open for God's future.

The model of revolution, furthermore, itself helps express the problem that "evolutionary development," social as well as natural, can work itself into blind alleys and thus develop "establishments" which restrict life development. For this reason it is unwise to equate the "spirit of an age" (even the revolutionary) with "God's spirit."

The problem with the pair "evolution/revolution" is that "evolution" is burdened with the biological past and does not really include conscious decision. Most extensions of the concept to include human consciousness distort, while retaining the dangerous mystique of being in some way "natural" as opposed to "arbitrary." But nature does not make ethical decisions (e.g., nature aborts spontaneously rather often, and brings "monsters" to term). It is man's responsibility to manipulate the laws of nature so that they serve the good of mankind rather than destroy it. Medicine has manipulated the laws of nature so that sickness no longer decimates the population at frequent intervals. There is nothing unnatural or arbitrary about seeking health, but there is something wrong when we do not then take measures to control the resulting birthrate and the quality of those births. This is not playing God, for God has never taken such responsibility away from man. It is responding to the God-given challenge of humanity. To do otherwise would be to use past theological models to shirk present responsibility.

When the word *revolution* is used to mean the opposite of *evolution* it tends to be understood as a sudden eruption born of the people's passions but formed by that which it negates. If a revolution is to be more than the exchange of the upper two classes it must be formed by a future goal and accompanied by a consciousness of freedom and future capable of living out new structures. Evolution and revolution therefore should not be used as opposites; rather, a third term is needed which can mediate and lead ahead.

The abortion problem illustrates some of these issues. At present in the Western world abortion is used primarily by the emancipated as one of many tools to control birth problems and thus to help keep them emancipated. At the same time the unemancipated and oppressed in the Western world and in the Third World often do not even see a responsible use of abortion as a possibility. The oppressed women have been taught that their true and only nature is to procreate, i.e., nature decides and no conscious decision is allowable. When these women are kept away from other forms of creativity, it is no surprise to find them actively seeking fulfillment in bearing as many children as possible: they and their children remain oppressed. For these reasons many socialist countries provide abortions on demand, but the economy, though planned, was not programmed for adequate contraceptives and family planning was not adequately taught. Thus abortion became the only means of birth control and now there is considerable concern in medical circles about the harmful effects of multiple abortions.

Anything new must become thinkable before it is "makeable." Theologians and revolutionaries too often think that all they need do is preach that the "new aeon" has come. But the power of the word works more slowly than that. Perhaps it will always take a "radical fringe" to argue polemically on an issue in order to make any change possible. At any rate, those who were totally against contraception ten years ago are presently arguing for contraception, against abortion. A similar change has taken place among those who were for contraception and opposed to abortion. Those who would criticize the "radicals" tend to forget this function of igniting a movement. The so-called moderate position has little influence on the establishment unless that establishment sees the moderate position as the only way to avoid the "chaos" of the radicals. This does not prove that the truth is always in the middle between two extremes, but it might indicate the need for the radicals to bring movement into the systems.

We need models to deal with reality. The models of evolution and revolution when used as opposites have serious limitations. Therefore I suggest the model of *provolution.* Provolution stresses the element of God's loving and forgiving *pro nobis,* "for" and "before" us, as a moving goal which gives us a dynamic orientation point and which requires on our part a constant correction of course. It is not expected that we shall ever attain this goal, but it is rather a dimension of orientation, devotion and hope, which makes the realization of "concrete utopia" possible.

Provolution includes all of nature and implies that in the future man must more consciously and responsibly steer

social and "natural" evolutionary development and revolu-
tionarily correct mistakes if necessary by planned mutations,
etc. It encourages man to develop his own and nature's
potential to the fullest in the direction of love, respect, and
freedom for all mankind. Man's nature is formed by the
past but open to God's future. Therefore the only thing
which is "natural" to man is his will and his ability to
organize and change structures. To deal with abortion in a
provolutionary way we must study the past and ask what
opens the way to God's future.

Biblical Themes and Abortion

The Bible does not deal with induced abortion in the
modern sense of the term. Nevertheless, there are different themes which have played decisive roles in the history
of Western thought about abortion which should be understood before one can judge the present situation. It has
been well said that the unity of the Bible establishes the
multiplicity of the church. Our question is no exception.

The Yahwist tradition in the early chapters of Genesis (second creation story) is the only one which deals
specifically with the relationship between God and human
life. God formed a man out of dust and breathed the breath
of life into him, making him a "living being" or "person"
(Gen. 2:7). Man was a "living being" not because of his
human shape, which was only dust, but because of his
divinely given breath. According to this tradition, which
is still used, there is no *human* life until after the first
breath is taken; and therefore induced abortion causes no
theoretical problems. However, breath is not a critical criterion for either life or death today.

The priestly tradition (first creation story), with its
theological concern for the transcendency of God, limited
the connection between God and man or nature exclu-
sively to God's creative word. This tradition tended to

locate the seat of life in the blood (cf. Gen. 9:4). This contradicts the Yahwist tradition and so has often been used against abortion. Indeed, Genesis 9:6 can be translated: "Whoever sheds the blood of man *in* man, his blood shall be shed. . . ." But this translation strains the original meaning.

All biblical traditions agree that God actively either opens or closes the womb; he brings the baby out of the womb; indeed, he can even cause miscarriage as a form of punishment. Thus the responsibility for having a birth or not is basically God's. The gift of life is like a loan which God can take back at any time (Deut. 32:39). The fact remains, however, that no matter how relevant these views may have been for the ancient world they can be dangerous today if not viewed in historical perspective.

The abortion debate has been influenced by two other general understandings of life which can also be found in the Bible. Movement in general and purposeful motion in particular were understood as life (cf. Gen. 7:21). Both of these understandings have been significant, for the concept of "quickening," i.e., when the mother first feels motion, was used in common law as the point where abortion was no longer allowed. In the course of legal history there were times when a pregnant woman's execution was stayed only if the embryo had already descended (i.e., purposeful motion).

One part of biblical law has played a critical role in the Western abortion debate. It has made it impossible for even the most conservative Jewish tradition to totally reject abortion. That text is Exodus 21:22ff. which deals with accidental abortions:

> When men strive together, and hurt a woman with child, so that there is a miscarriage, and yet no harm follows, the one who hurt her shall be fined, according as the woman's husband shall lay upon him; and he shall pay as the judges determine. If any harm follows, then you shall give life for life, eye for eye. . . .

This text implies that at that time the embryo was not considered as a person with rights, but rather as property of the father the loss of which incurred financial responsibility (but no more) on the part of the offender. Only if the mother died was there any question of murder which was a capital offense. Some present-day Jews still hold that the embryo is a part of the mother's body and as such not a person till parturition has started.

By the time of the Septuagint translation of the Old Testament there had obviously been considerable thought about the status of the embryo and the question of induced abortions. The Ezekiel text was not translated, but rather interpreted in line with the Hellenistic Jewish theological thought of that day. This interpretation marks another critical course correction for theology: "And if two men fight and hit a pregnant woman and her child comes out not fully formed he shall be forced to pay a penalty. . . . But if it is formed then he shall give life for life. . . ." At this point the human form became the criterion for a person who should not be murdered.

The early church took this to be the biblical position. When the Bible was translated into Latin it was discovered that the Hebrew Bible did not support this reading. The early Christian position was not changed, however, because the "course correction" taken by the Septuagint seemed closer to Christ's spirit which called believers to sacrifice themselves for one another and to care for the least of Christ's brethren. Yet neither the Christian church nor the Jewish tradition maintained this position. The Jewish tradition later made the Hebrew Scriptures their norm, but when Christian theologians began to be against all forms of abortion this distinction was considered "hairsplitting."

The New Testament makes no mention of abortion. Attempts to discover a condemnation of abortion in the condemnations of "medicine" as "sorcery" are not convincing, since the point of that condemnation was that when one went to a "sorcerer" he was seeking healing from a rival religion instead of from "the good physician."

Church History

The church had thus no biblical condemnation of abortion, but it did have a strong motivation to love "even the least" in a society which practiced abortion freely without the help of modern medicine. Abortion was seen as an offense to God's creative process at work in the womb. Later the interpretative model of the immortal and disembodied "soul" became more dominant. But its effect was not necessarily opposed to abortion. If the soul comes to the embryo at some time after conception (forty, seventy, or eighty days) as was believed, abortion before that was possible. "Ensoulment" at conception was put forward to solve this problem. Although this notion drew attention away from the fact of development, it could be used to support abortion for the embryo's own sake: baptism of the embryo could take place to save the soul eternally when there was danger that the embryo might not live until birth.

From the beginning then there was resistance in the Christian tradition to abortion. But the penalty for abortion has varied markedly. Indeed, a consistent and nearly total prohibition of abortion developed only in the Roman tradition and only there in the last two centuries. This was possible because of the rise of papal power and was due to the growing concern that scientific man was gaining control of nature in a way that threatened God's dominion. But even papal pronouncements that at conception the "embryo" is human to the same degree that its parents are have not been able to prohibit all abortions. Rome does accept abortions in the case of ectopic pregnancies or cancerous uteri. These exceptions are justified by the principle of "double effect," i.e., the death of the embryo is neither desired nor the goal of the operation. Both of these exceptions, and especially that of the cancerous uterus, show that the principle of inviolability has been broken and with it the theology of unique immortal souls. For if there were such an absolute principle, it would determine the question in isolation and there would be no exceptions, no drawing of lines.

The Present Problem

Man's evolutionary history has given him what has been a necessary potential and habit for prolific procreation. The modern world, however, has removed this necessity and thus turned the blessing of many children into a curse. Yet the forces which resist change are still present. Religious and cultural traditions have everywhere tended to teach women that their proper fulfillment is in bearing and rearing children. Medicine has made it possible to bear and sustain individuals who in an earlier age would have died—and who still die in certain parts of our present world. Technical society has removed the education of children from the home and alleviated most home tasks.

Childbirth should no longer be an automatic result of marriage. If women are "humanized," i.e., given the possibility of realizing their potentials in all areas of life, then there can be a conscious and free decision for or against procreation. Decisions concerning abortion should be well-informed, free, ethical decisions. Provolution stresses the social dimension of human nature and so would not leave the woman alone in her decision, i.e., she should be presented with viable options to abortion along with the means to carry them out. This would require considerable changes in most welfare systems. But there can be no "super-human judge figure" who makes the final decision for the women and her family. History shows that whenever such instances are set up many women refuse this "second rape" and opt for illegal abortions with all the danger that implies. If *ethical* decisions are desired, then *decisions* must be allowed.

Life, if we mean human life, must be viewed in contexts far wider than only the physical. Those who claim that any mother will eventually love her child regardless of how unwanted at first reduce the mother-child relationship to the animal level. They seem to forget that after the necessary physical care for the animal young has been accomplished the young are kicked out and treated as competition. This is not an adequate model for human behavior and when practiced does not manifest a reverence for human life. Reverence for human life involves, among other things, a loving and capable family in a society which encourages development.

There has also been considerable effort to oppose abortion on the basis of biological data. What is often forgotten here is that all data is already interpretation. The meaning of a word is its use in its context. "Human" can among other things mean a developed and mature person or a future goal for all of mankind, or it can mean simply a minimal biological difference from the lower animals, etc. Biologists have justly complained that their statements to the effect that the embryo has a human development from the very beginning are being misused when they are quoted to "prove" that abortion is biologically improper. Words are never absolute or constant metaphysical principles. Therefore it is not enough to ask when human life begins. There is not now nor has there ever been agreement on this question. The basis on which we determine our definition for a specific purpose will be more important for abortion decisions than the resultant definition.

It is no longer possible to claim that what is born of humans is necessarily human, because we know that sometimes natural developments within the womb go completely astray. Although ontogenesis apparently does not entail an ordered phylogenesis, as was once thought, there seem to be stages of development toward the level of the human which are not always reached. This observation has relevance for the timing of abortion, but the basic problem involved here will require more than abortion for a solution. Man is forced by his God-given potential for technical ability to take more and more responsibility for the occasion of human life and death. It is not ethical to take credit for his accomplishments and to blame God for technical and moral failures. If man is responsible for the occasion, he must also take the responsibility for correcting mistakes.

Those who fear that all moral dams will break if abortion decisions are set free forget that abortion is and always has been widely practiced. Once again the meaning of abortion is the use to which it is put. If it is used irresponsibly by a society it will be demonic; if it is used responsibly it can enhance the quality of life in the family and society.

Conclusion

This brief essay cannot go into a detailed analysis of how individual abortion decisions should be made. Suffice it to say here that all "indications" document failure in our society as much as in an individual. Christians have an obligation to work toward a society in which social and humanitarian indications will be extremely rare. We must also work for medical advance which will make medical, fetal, and psychiatric indications less frequent. This would be a society with neither compulsory pregnancy nor compulsory abortion.

Provolution is *pro* individual (mother, father, and potential child), *pro* society (family and larger social units), and *pro* future. Abortion is not the critical issue as many would make it today. It is neither a cure-all nor the end of all morals. Those who have been traditionally radically opposed to abortion have not worked for a social system which would make abortion unnecessary. There is the danger that after we have set abortion decisions free many will see the problem as solved. Provolution cannot see abortion as an escape from responsibility, but rather as a possible step toward more responsibility. Theology has had to correct course many times in order to keep the dynamic goal in sight, i.e., to develop new thought and social structures which enlarge the probability of free and responsible decisions for God's future.

DOING THEOLOGY FOR THE
SAKE OF RADICAL CHANGE

T. RICHARD SNYDER

It strikes some people as strange that someone committed to radical socio-economic and political change should spend time doing theology. As one who spends his time this way, I confess to having my doubts at times. For me, specifically, the temptation is to view our age apocalyptically and to assume that all time spent in anything other than action is wasted.

But a sober look at the "movement" in which I have participated in a variety of ways reveals that there is a great need for direction and new resources. What has happened in many situations is that movement has been replaced by frantic activity, repetitive strategies, fragmentation, ineffective action, and inhuman behavior. We cannot assume that the movement for social change needs no other resources than those which have been operative to this point.

Even granting this, however, there is serious reason to question whether the Judeo-Christian heritage can offer any resources at this time. First of all, for increasing numbers of people the heritage is bankrupt, it no longer carries any weight, because our beliefs, for the most part, have been associated with "religious" actions. As long as religious actions were part of the warp and woof of the life of our society in general, faith seemed relevant. Now, in an increasingly secular age, these actions and, therefore, the beliefs which led to them, appear vacuous. We face a crisis of faith and works because many of us no longer know what it means to be a Christian.

This was brought home to me forcibly on a recent trip to Cuba, one of the most overtly secular nations in the West. Much of the church there is in a state of shock. It is not that Christians have given up their faith; quite the opposite. There is an almost frantic nostalgia about the significance of the gospel and the church, a kind of inarticulate feeling that the faith is correct and somehow will endure. But, while many are convinced that the Christian faith is still alive and has something to offer, most are no longer sure just what that means. The problem is that they simply do not know what to believe or do. They have not been able to discover, in concrete terms, what it means to be a Christian in the midst of a society which rejects all religion but, at the same time, accomplishes many of the tasks to which the church has felt and does feel itself called. Because they are unable to discover what the nature of the church's mission in a secular society should be, they are confused and immobilized. Perhaps the only difference between the church in Cuba and the church in the United States is that things in Cuba are in a more advanced stage. But it is the same crisis.

Many of us who have been part of the "movement" in the last five or ten years have discovered that we have little to add from our heritage except a few symbolic trappings, such as an occasional fast or, less frequently, the celebrations of the Catonsville Nine. The struggle is too complex to assume that we can draw upon our heritage to rescue the halting attempts at social change. On the other hand, it would be equally naive to pretend that the movement for social change in our nation and world is not in desperate need of resources from many quarters.

What the Religious Revolutionaries Are Saying

The job of discovering resources from our Judeo-Christian heritage is no simple matter. Metropolitan Associates of Philadelphia (MAP) has had a number of worker-ministers as part of its experiment in developing a ministry of the laity within secular institutions. These men are all theologically trained and some have spent as much as three and one-half years attempting to discover the relationship between their faith and their secular involvements. It is the exception who has been able to make even the most superficial of connections. The dilemma of the worker-minister is one sign among many of the crisis in our theology.

The essential problems, as I see things, are two. First, most contemporary theologies provide little or no connection between theory and practice, especially if the practice relates to secular social change. Second, most theological resources are redundant: that is, they are after the fact and frequently do only what others are already doing better.

Some theologies guarantee a lack of relationship between the faith and social change. Among them is the approach which begins with a system of ideas removed from experience. When you operate out of a rational construct the contradictions and exigencies of history can be ignored. They are subsumed under something which is beyond history and nature.

This is the way God functions for many of us. We suppose an eternal realm quite beyond all the problems of our existence and unaffected by them. There is no essential connection between the two realms, only an occasional one. Karl Barth's theology seems to many younger theologians to be the greatest contemporary example of such an approach. God chooses to touch history only tangentially at certain key moments.

The problem with this approach is that reason is cut off from reality. To have a closed system of revelation which operates in a realm different from our history means that we cannot treat the history we live with real seriousness. That sort of revelational theology offers us no critical tools for dealing with the struggle for social transformation.

An even more fundamental problem is the assumption that there can be a rational structure of reality. I believe Herbert Marcuse and others are correct: there is no such thing. In fact, what many have assumed to be the true order of reality is actually a chosen and historically conditioned way of putting things together—and this changes with history.

Sometimes the lack of unity of theory and practice is contrary to the intention of theology. For example, there are a number of theologies which have developed intricate and exhaustive lists of directions for living. They intend to offer resources for us. The casuistry of some of the Thomists and most Protestant fundamentalists are cases in point. While these theologies attempt to provide specific answers to all situations, they fail. They fail because they assume an eternally similar historical situation in which truths for one time are thought to be applicable for all times. As Paul Lehmann points out, such a view ignores the struggle of the early church concerning the canon of Scripture, a struggle which would not have been necessary if some system or some specific collection of writings had been self-evidently authoritative for all time. Any theology which attempts to make answers from the past apply to all present and future situations is guaranteed to be irrelevant. History changes.

Probably the most prevalent way of doing theology today, by those concerned about social change, leads to redundancy. Many of us have tended to become amateur social scientists who analyze the social scene and then attempt to describe it in theological categories. The danger of this method is its arbitrary use of the past and the tendency for dogmas to develop in competition, based upon differing social analyses. Rather than theology serving as a resource, it provides the rationalization or justification for a particular course of action. Harvey Cox's *Secular City* is an example of this kind of approach.

One reason for the redundancy is that this type of theology frequently accepts the questions as posed by sociology and other sciences. This dare not be. A major problem today is that we have not explored the fullness of most of the questions; hence, we are getting inadequate answers.

Each of these major ways of doing theology today falls into the trap of subsuming one under the other. In the first two cases, the contemporary struggle is subsumed under a rational system or an infallible list of directions. In the third case, the heritage is subsumed under the current culture. We need a method which holds the contemporary situation and the heritage in tension so that each can help to shape the other.

I do not pretend to have worked out a new way of doing theology. What follows are some pieces of a theological method growing out of the reflection and work a few of us in Philadelphia have been doing together.

There are at least three critical factors that need to be dealt with: context, language, and method.

Context. Theology must go on in the context of action. That means not that a theologian must always be acting but that the issues, problems, and opportunities raised by an action context are necessary as a first step. It is the absence of an action context which makes most seminary (and other professional) education so unrelated to reality.

The nature of that action is critical. All too often we limit the contexts to which we relate our theological reflection to religious types of action. For example, field-work assignments for most seminarians are in church school programs and youth groups. I believe it essential that anyone seeking to do theology for the sake of signifi-

Theology and Change

cant social change must be involved directly in the struggle for that change.

Of course, that presents problems. Any of us who have attempted this find ourselves in a bind. On the one hand the action demands in themselves are sufficient to consume all our time. On the other hand, time spent in study and thought is frequently not valued by activists and we are pressured (often by guilt) to get with the action. There may be a few rare persons who can maintain a balance within themselves between action and reflection. For the majority who cannot, this raises another point about the proper context for doing theology: it needs to be communal.

The day of the isolated, individual scholar is past, perhaps with a few exceptions. If sharing in the struggle for change is critical, then one way to do that is to be part of a struggling community. This means sharing with others the risks, concerns, and work. It also means being in a community which values the reflective work you are trying to do. In this kind of a community the chances for parochialism are diminished and questions can be pushed to the fullest and the struggle for new directions can be a joint one.

Increasingly, it is impossible to do the kind of study and thinking that is necessary as an individual. The issues and problems raised in our struggle are too vast, changing too rapidly, and too complex to be handled by one person. We need now to experiment with a team-scholarship in which a number of persons define a problem for study and then take a piece of it for full study.

Language. While I am not a linguist, the question of language is critical. There are at least two ways to handle the language problem. The first is to reinterpret and thus recapture the original meaning. There are certain words which are rich in historical meaning that may be recov-

145

erable. But reinterpretation involves several things, including a similarity of experience between that which the word originally described or symbolized and that of the contemporary hearer. Further, it generally presupposes some familiarity with the words in the first place. Assuming that at least the latter is true, old words can take on new (or recover original) meanings by changing the event or thing about which they speak. That is what the Blacks have done with the word *black*. What was once a proud and beautiful designation (cf., e.g., Song of Solomon) had become in our society a term of scorn and derision. But, by association with beautiful or exemplary events, the term has begun to recapture some of its original usage. The same thing must happen to a word like *reconciliation*, which has come to mean a smoothing over of differences through dialogue, patience, and understanding. The reintroduction of suffering and struggle into the meaning of that word comes about as we apply the name to events and actions, as the Berrigans have done with their destruction of draft files.

While reinterpretation of old theological language may be possible for those who have some familiarity with that language, there is an increasing number of persons, especially among the young, for whom the words have no meaning at all. It may be that this offers the possibility of introducing these words in a fresh way. I do not discount that possibility. But more likely we shall have to use another language which communicates to them. We are increasingly faced with the problem of reinventing language rather than reinterpreting it.

Methodology. The method I am using is dialectical. It involves a constant alternation between the contemporary situation and the heritage, so that each continuously shapes and informs the other. As my critique of existing theologies would indicate, I reject starting from some point within a revelatory or metaphysical system. We have to start where we are, where our commitments are being played out. We start with an existential wager, a wager about what it is that is worth working for. Of course, that wager is made not in isolation nor by a mere flip of the coin. For each of us, it is shaped by our present context and our history. In other words, the wager is communally and historically conditioned. Each of us is actually living out of wagers about reality—wagers about what is important, what is lasting, what is fulfilling.

For some, that wager is that life is a competitive rat race in which only the hardworking can succeed. This is best seen in the Puritan work ethic. For others, the wager is that white men find fulfillment in acting out their superiority over Blacks. These wagers fundamentally shape our lives: the way we spend our time, the questions we raise, the glasses through which we view our society.

For many who are part of both the historical Judeo-Christian community and the movement for social change, the wager is that life is all about human liberation. What makes most sense to us is to share in the struggle to transform our own lives and that of our society, a transformation from the bondages which prevent our fulfillment as persons both individually and interrelatedly.

To say that, of course, may be merely a shibboleth, a jargon phrase which one tunes in or out depending upon his predisposition. In order to move beyond rhetoric we need to unpack the meaning of that phrase concretely. And to do so, we need to do an analysis of the pieces, issues, and problems which the word *liberation* entails.

Such an analysis is the next stage in our method. We begin with a wager, a wager which grows out of our communal and action context. We then move to an understanding of all that is involved in that wager. Without a careful and thorough analysis at this stage, we are liable to fall into an overly simplistic understanding of the problem and thus of the solutions. We have found that such an analysis must be interdisciplinary if it is to uncover both the breadth and the specifics of what needs to occur.

Liberation certainly entails the provision of basic material needs for all persons, the liberation from physical and economic deprivation and exploitation. But to stop with a purely economic analysis and solution fails to deal with other basic components of liberation today, such as participation. Liberation entails maximum participation in the decisions which affect our lives, or liberation from unchosen, external control. And it also entails what Marcuse calls the "eroticization" of life, the liberation of the whole self from the bondage of one dimensional existence. And it means the possibility of a pluralism of values and life-styles consonant with the above.

To allow the economist or the psychologist or the theologian to tell us what liberation must be is to guarantee a reduction of the problem and, consequently, a superficial liberation. We have found that it is in the dialogue of various perspectives that the intricacies and fullness of the problem are understood. And that dialogue can take place at every level. For example, one of the specific pieces in the struggle for liberation today is the attempt to maximize the participation of all persons in the decisions which affect them. The overt colonial status in which Blacks, Browns, and poor Whites live in our society and the more covert status in which most of us live cannot continue. The press for participation is coming from every quarter. But it is one thing to assert this and quite another to understand both what the shape of that participation should be and how to bring it about.

We need to understand the psychological needs of both the controller and the controlled. For example, what are the self-interest factors at work which might make it easier for the controller to yield the power which he has? What counterrewards can be developed? What about the colonized person who has had decisions made for him so long that he has no desire to participate? What happens if he is given power without the desire to have it?

The problems are not only psychological, of course. Nonparticipation is maintained by economic and educational systems which reward and train persons to fit the role of colonizer or colonized, cultural myths which provide rationalizations for the status quo, organizational forms which perpetuate the old and co-opt moves toward participation.

Almost every significant change needed within our society is systemic. In order to understand the complexities and interrelationships of these various systems, we have found it necessary to do careful interdisciplinary analysis. Without that we are reduced, at best, to moralizing, which results in increased guilt or in the feeling of having accomplished something merely by talking about it. Or we are reduced to simplistic and partial solutions which function as placebos, sugar pills which make us feel like we're doing something, but which allow the disease to run unchecked.

The next element in the process is to go to our heritage (whether biblical studies, church history, systematic theology, ethics) in order to probe the questions more deeply and to seek clues as to how to move ahead. The method for dealing with that history is necessarily selective. We need to go back to those moments, events, and statements in our heritage which we suspect may grow out of a predicament similar to ours. This is quite different from having a ready-made answer and then finding proof for it. What I am suggesting is that we go back to those points where we suspect that a similar dilemma has been faced. This method does not deny the existence of other important dilemmas in the heritage but it selects those which appear germane to our situation.

A word of caution is in order here. Since one of the most consistent facts about our heritage is its ability to surprise us, we need to be in touch with the broadest possible number of persons working theologically. Others may help us to discover the unexpected. We dare not get locked into our narrow program of studies and expectations. Here again the need for a reflective community is critical.

If the situation we face is one of political, economic, and social bondage and the wager we make is for liberation, then the moments to which we look might be the Exodus, prophetic nationalism, the revolt of the Maccabees, Jesus' relationship to the Jewish and Roman religious-political complex, the radical Reformation, the Puritan revolution, etc. The fact that the events and points to which we turn are not the dominant motifs with the heritage is unimportant. We are looking not for dominance or orthodoxy but for similar dilemmas.

One evening, in dealing with the question of participation with some managers, the question of when people have earned the right to participate was raised. This generated some discussion. It struck me that here was a case of an inadequate question. Given the assumption behind the question, the person currently in power decides when the powerless have earned the right to power.

I was reminded of the almost constant struggle for participation which characterized the life of Israel, beginning with its birth struggle in Egypt. One of the moments in Israel's history when the struggle for participation was most acute occurred in the early days of monarchy. The people asked for a king like the other nations. Saul was designated king and given virtual carte blanche over the people. But, as his actions turned against the values of the nation he was rejected and David was chosen to replace him. The people participated in choosing and unchoosing.

While Israel constantly was tempted to be like the other nations and often yielded to that temptation, the thing that continually distinguished it from others was its active participation in shaping its own history. Jews believed that it was their right to exercise power. They could choose a new king and overthrow the old.

What gives people this open stance toward participation? From the records about Israel, I would conclude that it was two things. First, Israel participated in choosing; therefore they could unchoose. The choice was a historical event, not something mysteriously given and unalterable. The oldest part of the narrative indicates that while some people wanted Saul for king, this was resisted for a time. The thing which turned all the people to him was his successful military leadership in a decisive battle. After that, they agreed to make him the king. Such a recognition of the historical nature of the kingship (as opposed to the mythical) desacralizes the kingship. I suspect that the situation is similar today. One of the basic motivations for participation is a realization of a nonfatalistic nature of existence; a perception of history as being man-made. If man has shaped what is, he can change it.

The second factor in Israel's freedom to choose a new king was its belief in a higher authority. Saul had been anointed by Samuel. Saul's leadership depended upon his loyalty and faithfulness to something (or someone) which transcended the narrow limits of his own desires and his own reading of the situation. Again, this desacralized the authority of the king. There can be no absolute authority for those who recognize the transcendence which permeates history.

It was these thoughts which helped to call into question the basic premises of the discussion we were having. In our society the question "When have people earned the right to participate?" is a tool of the oppressor. The people always have the right to participate, since authority is historically made and is not absolute. The real question is this: "Is the authority which is being exercised a delegated, chosen authority?" If it is not, then it has no right to exist. The other question which needs to be asked is: "Is that authority existing as if it were absolute?" If it is, it has no right to exist.

In this case, the heritage can help us both to understand the complexity of the problems and to discover some possible ways to move when we encounter a tyrannical authority. It may be that many others could have suggested similar questions and directions. Certainly many political scientists have dealt with the man-made nature of systems and powers, and therefore the possibility of changing them. I make no claims of uniqueness for theology.

There are many other questions which must be dealt with in regard to the struggle for participation. What is the shape of the new power distribution if we wish to avoid simply a power shift in which a previously oppressed group now becomes the oppressors? How can the movement for participation be kept from elitism if the nonparticipants have been trained in docility? What is legitimate power? These questions force us back to the heritage in a new way, asking questions of it that have not been asked and shaping the heritage in different ways.

The process is a continuous one, a dialectic in which both the questions and answers are being reshaped, a process in which the contemporary situation and the heritage are interacting, reshaping and informing each other. Anything less than this kind of a dialectical process will treat the present too superficially and too statically.

CONTRIBUTORS

Stephen S. Dixon, a Presbyterian clergyman, is a graduate student in ethics in the Department of Religion of Temple University in Philadelphia. He has also studied at Bonn, Germany, the Pittsburgh Theological Seminary, and the University of California at Los Angeles.

John R. Fry is a minister at the First Presbyterian Church in the Woodlawn section of Chicago. His work with the inner-city gang known as the "Blackstone Rangers" has occupied much of his ministry and he is the author of *Fire and Blackstone.*

Arthur Gilbert is Dean of the newly-formed Reconstructionist Rabbinical College, which is linked with the Department of Religion at Temple University. He is also Adjunct Professor of Religion and Sociology at Marymount Manhattan College in New York and the author of *A Jew in Christian America* and *The Vatican Council and the Jews.*

David M. Gracie is Urban Missioner for the Diocese of Pennsylvania of the Protestant Episcopal Church. A veteran of the U.S. Army, he attended the Episcopal Theological School in Cambridge, Massachusetts, and was for six years a parish priest in Detroit, Michigan.

John W. Groutt is an instructor in religion and psychology on leave from Villanova University, Villanova, Pennsylvania. A graduate of St. Vincent College in Latrobe, Pennsylvania, he also studied at Gregorian University in Rome.

A. Theodore Kachel is Director of the Office of Religious Affairs for the University of Michigan, Ann Arbor. His doctorate was taken at Union Theological Seminary and Columbia University in New York City, and he was formerly Secretary for College Relationships for the Board for Homeland Ministry of the United Church of Christ.

153

Edward L. Lee, Jr., a graduate of Brown University and General Theological Seminary in New York City, is Episcopal Advisor to the University Christian Movement at Temple University. He is presently national chairman of the Episcopal Peace Fellowship.

Elwyn A. Smith is Professor of Religion and Vice-President for Student Affairs of Temple University in Philadelphia. He is the editor of *The Religion of the Republic,* also published by Fortress Press in 1971, which is a major symposium on the question of the "American civil religion."

T. Richard Snyder is theologian on the staff of Metropolitan Associates of Philadelphia, an action/research project concerned with institutional change in American society. His doctorate is from Princeton Theological Seminary and he formerly taught at Rutgers University and did research in Cuba and Latin America.

Joseph C. Williamson taught for six years at the Andover Newton Theological School before resigning in 1970 to work full time in the counterculture. He is currently affiliated with the work collective of Cambridge (Massachusetts) Ministries in Higher Education, Project Place, and the New Community Seminary in Boston.

Richard Shaull is Henry W. Luce Professor of Ecumenics at Princeton Theological Seminary. He is chairman of the World's Student Christian Federation and of the North American Congress on Latin America. He is co-author, with Carl Oglesby, of *Containment and Change: Two Dissenting Views of American Society and Foreign Policy in the New Revolutionary Age.*

James E. Woodruff is Executive Director of the Union of Black Clergy and Laity, the national Black caucus of the Protestant Episcopal Church. A lecturer in theology at the Princeton Theological Seminary and a contributor to the anthology *The Underground Church,* he is presently on a leave of absence from the staff of the Diocese of Pennsylvania.